T0016842

Bedtime Devotions for Peaceful Sleep

VALORIE QUESENBERRY

Bedtime Devotions for Peaceful Sleep

6 MONTHS OF DAILY BLESSINGS
for Women

BARBOUR
PUBLISHING

Published by Barbour Publishing, Inc., 1810 Barbour Drive, Uhrichsville, Ohio 44683, www.barbourbooks.com

Our mission is to inspire the world with the life-changing message of the Bible.

 Member of the
Evangelical Christian
Publishers Association

Printed in China.

When you lie down,
you will not be afraid;
when you lie down,
your sleep will be sweet.

PROVERBS 3:24 NIV

Introduction

I may be the most unlikely person ever to write a book pertaining to bedtime.

Frankly, I struggle with bedtime. Since I enjoy social interaction and could probably be labeled a "night owl," I don't view the approaching isolation of sleep with delight. In fact, my mood often swings to introspection and even melancholy.

But many people are eager to lie down at night. They crave their sleep and enjoy every minute of it. And then there are those people who look forward to rest but for whatever reason can't sleep. Their nights become frustrating.

Whatever your case may be, you can know this: our loving Father in heaven created sleep for our good. Even before the world was cursed and twisted by sin, He instituted evening and morning, the sun to rule the day and the moon and stars the night. From the very beginning, it seems that human beings were designed to rest during the dark hours. And God called everything He designed "good."

The nighttime is His reset button for our minds and bodies. And I think we all feel better after a good night's sleep, don't we?

So, in this little book, we're going to explore this gift from our loving Creator. We'll see what His Word has to say about it and how we can use it in the best way possible. We're going to quiet our hearts and minds and focus on the One who watches over our sleep. Aren't you ready for that? I know I am.

Section 1:
GET YOUR ZZZZS
THE OTHER PART

God called the light Day, and the darkness he called Night.
And the evening and the morning were the first day.
GENESIS 1:5 KJV

No day is complete without its night.

If you're like me, you tend to think of day and night as separate events, but they're actually two halves of a whole—at least according to the One who created them. The God of the universe chose to design this piece of time called *day* and to include in it both light and darkness. Knowing that He would create humankind to inhabit the earth, He decided to give us a period of darkness in which to recharge and rest. Think about it! Before fallenness entered our world, nighttime was part of God's plan.

I don't know how life would differ if the first humans hadn't rebelled and brought a curse on everything. Surely we would not experience the negative things many people associate with nighttime—fatigue, body aches, irritability, melancholy. However, it does seem that God built into us (and into the rhythm of our world) the need for a time of renewal. He designed the night. It's good because He made it for us.

. . . .

Heavenly Father, thank You for creating the nighttime for
me. Give me the maturity to see it not as an interruption
of my day but as an important part of it. Amen.

NIGHT DECLARATIONS

*It is good to give thanks to the Lord, and to sing praises to
Your name, O Most High; to declare Your lovingkindness
in the morning, and Your faithfulness every night.*
PSALM 92:1–2 NKJV

You've probably heard the advice not to talk about serious matters late at night. For some reason, our ability to sort things out logically and rationally is not at its peak when we're tired! Ask any married couple—they will tell you that disagreements are likely to be more intense and harder to control at night. So it's best to have important discussions earlier in the day, when our minds are fresh and our emotions are balanced.

But one type of discussion is always appropriate, day or night. The writer of Psalm 92 begins with the reminder that giving thanks and singing praise have no set times.

The psalmist specifically says that it is good to declare the Lord's faithfulness every night. Now, this doesn't mean that God is more faithful at night than during the day. But I think the writer was divinely inspired to tell us to focus on God's faithfulness in the nighttime—when we are often tempted to worry and fret. In those dim hours, when problems loom large and solutions seem few, we must set our minds to lean on God's faithful character. And in that firm resolve, we will find rest.

. . . .

*Lord, I purpose now that I will declare Your faithfulness
in the night hours. In Jesus' name, amen.*

NO CORDS REQUIRED

The whole earth is at rest, and is quiet.

ISAIAH 14:7 KJV

I have a vivid memory of a video—titled *The Electric Grandmother*—that I watched as a child. Mixing actual life with fantasy, the writers had spun a story of a family whose mother had died, and who longed for a loving maternal figure in their home. They were put in touch with a company that provided grandmothers—but these elderly homemakers weren't quite human.

The family should have gotten a clue when "Grandma" was delivered in a type of sarcophagus lowered to the ground by helicopter. But their lives were wonderfully changed with her arrival. She made cookies, kept the house sparkling and homey, sang them to sleep, and gave them lots of affection. One night, one of the children went to investigate an unusual noise, only to find Grandmother in the basement, plugged into the wall outlet! Her rocking chair was moving rhythmically to the sounds of her digital system being updated and recharged.

Thankfully, you and I don't have to position our beds close to electrical sockets! But our bodily systems do need to be updated and our minds reset. As you lay down to rest tonight, give in to the reboot that God has scheduled just for you. And be glad you don't have to worry about accidentally unplugging yourself.

. . . .

Father in heaven, I need to be recharged tonight. Give my body rest, and bring peace to my spirit. In Jesus' name, amen.

AWARDS NIGHT

*Every man should eat and drink and enjoy the
good of all his labor—it is the gift of God.*

ECCLESIASTES 3:13 AMPC

Every year, our family looks forward to a particular night in May: awards night at school. When this evening comes, we rejoice.

One reason is because it signals we have reached the end of the school year. For Mom that means a break from packing lunches, ironing uniforms, and driving the family "bus" two times a day. For the students, it means long summer evenings and no homework.

Another reason we anticipate this night is the possibility of rewards for the diligence and patient academic suffering of the previous ten months.

In a similar way, I think *every* night should be awards night for us as humans. God places a premium on positive activity—our purposeful work. Even before the Fall, He gave duties to the first human couple, and still today He wants us to be appropriately engaged in work. After that, He wants us to feel the reward of accomplishment when our work is done. I think God smiles on family mealtimes, our evening walks, and time on the porch or deck together. And I'm pretty sure He wants our bedtime to be a sweet reward for the hard labor of the daylight hours.

. . . .

*Father God, You created both work and rest. The Bible tells
me that You did both in the beginning. I ask You to help
me work hard and rest well. For Your glory, amen.*

LULLABIES AT NIGHT

"Where is God my Maker, who gives songs in the night?"
JOB 35:10 ESV

Brahms didn't create the lullaby.

It might seem so, since his classic melody is instantly associated with babies and sweet slumber. But there is another who gave us song in the first place, the One who gave the stars their cosmic notes and the whales their aquatic melodies. Our God is the God of all music, for every good and perfect gift is from above, we are told in James 1:17.

There is music throughout creation, even in the nighttime. The gentle rhythm of the wind, the lap of the ocean on a moonlit beach, the howl and hoot of nocturnal creatures, the buzz of insects in the summer darkness—all are part of the night noise that lulls our minds and bodies to sleep.

But more than that, there is music in our souls. The glad refrain of grace and forgiveness in Christ, the continual chorus of praise for the person and work of our God, the pounding lines of scriptural promises which are the soundtrack for our lives—these are the songs He gives us for the nighttime. And it is never too dark to enjoy them.

. . . .

Heavenly Father, thank You for creating music—especially songs in the night. Let me sing them to You tonight. Amen.

NIGHT MUSINGS

His delight is in the law of the LORD,
and in His law he meditates day and night.

PSALM 1:2 NKJV

What fills our minds at night is often what dominates us. Our cravings for significance and acceptance and love rise to the top when we are tired and depleted of the energy to think rationally. Addictions can be most active in the night hours, and the heart goes to its default setting when fatigue takes over. In these raw moments, the habits and thoughts that define us are unleashed.

But the psalmist declares that the blessed man (or woman!) meditates on the law of the Lord both day and night. To "meditate" is to focus the mind on something for an extended time. Addictions demand control of the mind; godly meditation guards the mind. Our Creator knows that our minds are key to our behavior, so He tells us often in scripture to meditate on things that bring us close to Him. Godly patterns of thought are helpful not only in maintaining personal integrity but also in developing pure joy in living. Blessed people are so hungry to know God intimately that they muse on the Word both day and night—this is their continual routine.

Lord, develop in me a deep hunger for Your law. Help me
learn how to meditate on it continually. Amen.

HE HOLDS IT

The day is Yours, the night also is Yours;
You have prepared the light and the sun.

PSALM 74:16 NKJV

Too often I think of the day as *mine*. You know what the store **clerk says to you** as she hands you the receipt for your purchase: "Enjoy **your day!**" And I think what she means is, "Take pleasure in what you're doing **today.** Feel** happy as you do what you do." It's all about me, right?

But, in reality, my day belongs to God. Psalm 139:16 tells us that **all our days were** "fashioned" for us by Him and every one of them is **numbered for us in** His record. That goes for my nights too. They are all His.

In Psalm 74:16, Asaph acknowledged God as the owner of both **day and night**—not only of Asaph's days and nights, but of the very *idea* of **day and night.** Having "prepared the light and the sun," God could control **even the degree** of light and darkness in each.

As you fall back on your pillow tonight, remember that **the moonlight outside your** window is set **by the** One who created and **controls it all. And** go to sleep comforted.

. . . .

Creator God, thank You for holding the universe and the solar
system in Your hands. I rest in Your care tonight. Amen.

IT'S ONLY SLEEPING

When [Jesus] came in, He said to them, "Why make this
commotion and weep? The child is not dead, but sleeping."
MARK 5:39 NKJV

When our children are little and learning how to pray, we sometimes teach them this rhyming prayer:

Now I lay me down to sleep; I pray Thee, Lord, my soul to keep.
If I should die before I wake, I pray Thee, Lord, my soul to take.

Some have suggested this classic rhyme is too morbid for children, creating fear that they might die in their sleep. But the wording of the poem also touches on an important truth: for the Christian, physical death is like sleep.

Jesus taught this in the Bible verse above, from the story of His raising of Jairus' daughter from death; He said the same thing about Lazarus whom He also brought back to life. Acts 7:60 says that Stephen, the first Christian martyr, "fell asleep," and the apostle Paul referred to Christians in the grave awaiting resurrection as "those who sleep in Jesus" (1 Thessalonians 4:14 NKJV). Because Christ conquered death for us, we can see it as simply a time of sleep for our earthly bodies—while our living souls go immediately into His presence.

. . . .

Jesus, thank You for being the Victor over death and the grave.
You hold the keys to them both. I fall asleep in You tonight. Amen.

MIRACLES IN THE NIGHT

And God did so that night; and it was dry on the fleece
only, and on all the ground there was dew.

JUDGES 6:40 ESV

Have you heard the expression "putting out a fleece"?

It comes from an Old Testament story about Gideon, who was trying to figure out if God was really talking to him. Since Gideon didn't trust his own perceptions and was fearful of making a mistake in leading the army, he asked the Lord for a special sign. And God answered.

Sometimes, miracles happen in the night. God can change hearts, heal relationships, and restore balance to families. He walks in hospital corridors at midnight, stands by the moonlit beds of widows and abandoned children, and visits prisons and drug houses, offering redemption. He can work in the twenty-first century's darkness just as He did in Gideon's.

Now, I've heard it wisely explained by pastors and teachers that we should not expect to use this test in our own spiritual journeys—God does not "perform" according to our whims. Though He granted Gideon reassurance in this way, He is looking for faith on our part. But it's a faith in an all-knowing, all-powerful God who loves us dearly.

As the stars come out tonight, know this: whatever your crisis, it is not too difficult for God's amazing power.

. . . .

Lord, You are the Miracle Worker. Tonight, I bring You my specific need,
asking You to do what only You can do. In Jesus' name I pray, amen.

STORM SLEEPING

So they set out, and as they sailed [Jesus] fell asleep.
And a windstorm came down on the lake, and they
were filling with water and were in danger.
LUKE 8:22–23 ESV

I don't like to sleep during storms. When I close the blinds in my bedroom and pull back the sheets, I prefer a calm and peaceful night outside. Having lived near tornado-prone areas of Alabama and the Midwest, I am a bit paranoid about disaster striking in the middle of the night. There is nothing quite as startling as a sudden announcement on the weather radio or the screaming of a storm siren.

Startling and sudden seems to be the way this storm arose on the Sea of Galilee one evening when Jesus and His disciples were crossing. Jesus *was* asleep during the storm, and the crashing of His creation caused Him no anxiety whatsoever. After His disciples woke Him, Jesus simply spoke to the waves and the wind, and they instantly calmed.

I may never be okay with the idea of sleeping in a storm. But I'm going to make sure I stay close to the One who speaks peace, anytime of the day or night.

. . . .

Lord Jesus, You are the Master of the storm. Calm the
anxious winds blowing in my life tonight. Amen.

TEARS ON MY PILLOW

Weeping may go on all night, but in the morning there is joy.
PSALM 30:5 TLB

How many times have I cried into my pillow?

I don't remember. Quite a few. Nighttime amplifies feelings of loneliness and despair, the idea that the present situation is probably the worst one ever and there is no solution. At night, normal difficulties become monstrous—and there is nothing quite as melancholy as lying on your side of the bed (or maybe all alone in bed), isolated in your problems. I've felt that way often.

This verse praises God for rescuing the writer from his despair, giving thanks for the Lord's holy character. In the first part of verse 5, the psalmist says that God's anger lasts for a moment, but His favor endures for a lifetime. Then he mentions nighttime crying followed by joy in the morning.

While there are deep truths here related to God's character and our redemption, I think we may also apply this concept to our own emotions. However black the night seems—however dark our situation at present—the morning brings new opportunities for grace and help. God's mercies are new every morning (Lamentations 3:22–23). He is the God of hope and new beginnings.

. . . .

Father of hope, fill me tonight with the assurance that You can redeem whatever I bring to You. In Jesus' name, amen.

WHILE YOU SLEEP

And when the dew fell on the camp in the night, the manna fell on it.
NUMBERS 11:9 NKJV

Lots of things happen when we sleep, some good and some **bad**. It's **easy to forget that God is** awake all the time. He exists in a kind of **eternal light bubble. Things** don't seem different to Him whether it's noon or **midnight.** He works **without** change around the clock.

The ancient Hebrew people learned this truth in an incredible **way while they wandered in the** desert outside Canaan. They were hungry. **They were complaining. (Again.)** And God was merciful. He provided food **while they were sleeping. As** easily as He sent dew, He provided manna **with it. Not exactly fast food,** but better: perfectly created, perfectly **nutritious, perfectly delivered. When** the people woke up, there it was.

We need to be reminded that God can use any method He **wants to provide for us. And He might** decide to make His move in the night **hours, while we're sleeping.** Nothing is too difficult for Him. If He needs **to drop the answer from** the sky, He can do that. The key for us is to **trust—that whatever we** need to accomplish His purpose tomorrow will **be provided. Then leave the** delivery details with Him.

. . . .

Heavenly Father, thank You for providing what I need to do Your will.
Send it in whatever way You think is best. In Jesus' name, amen.

TAKE THE GIFT

*In vain you rise early and stay up late, toiling for food
to eat—for he grants sleep to those he loves.*
PSALM 127:2 NIV

Some see sleep as an escape.

Some see sleep as an inconvenience.

Some see sleep as an assignment.

God sees sleep as a gift.

After all, He created sleep. For our good. And this verse says **He gives
it to us** out of love.

Sleep is the body's time to recoup energy and renew its system. **Just as
our digital** devices need to have their operating systems and applications
updated, our bodies and minds need some downtime for improvement too.
I've already confessed that I'm not the greatest at this. But just as I **struggle
with** appreciating the benefits of sleep, others struggle with indulging **in
too much.** There is danger in either approach.

Our Creator wants balance in our perspective. He wants us to **embrace
and use** this gift but not to refuse the other blessings He **gives at other
times.** Tonight, as you lie down to sleep, appreciate this **gift of rest for
what it is:** a tool to be used for His ultimate glory. God is **giving your mind
and body the chance to operate** at maximum capacity for the purpose He
has for you tomorrow.

. . . .

*Heavenly Father, I acknowledge my need of rest and thank
You for the gift of it. Restore me while I sleep so I may
glorify You better tomorrow. In Jesus' name, amen.*

IT MIGHT SHOW ON YOUR FACE

The look on their countenance witnesses against them.
ISAIAH 3:9 NKJV

I wasn't sure I heard her right at first.

I was having lunch with a friend who works in a dermatology office. We were casually discussing her job and the types of skin disorders she sees, and my friend said that acne was the most common reason for patients' visits. And as we talked about causes of acne, she listed "lack of sleep."

That was news to me, but a brief internet search turned up more details. Lack of sleep causes stress in the body, causing the skin to secrete more sebum—which in turn results in a flare-up of acne. In the same way, lack of sleep increases the production of proinflammatory cytokines in the blood, causing generalized inflammation in the body.

Who knew?

Well, God did. I'm not saying that complexion problems were His primary concern in creation, but He did put our body systems into balance so that one thing affects another. So, tonight, use your medicated facial wash and smear on your special gels. . .but also make sure you're laying that face on the pillow at a good time. The benefits might surprise you.

. . . .

Lord, You put everything on earth into rhythm—even our body chemistry. Tonight, I ask You to help me be a good steward of my health by investing in proper sleep. Amen.

AFTER-HOURS DISPLAY

The heavens declare the glory of God; and the firmament
shows and proclaims His handiwork.
PSALM 19:1 AMPC

Most museums have hours of operation. And they're usually open to the public only in the daytime, during normal business hours.

But God runs His show a little differently. His stage is set 24-7 and nighttime is as amazing as daytime. He lets the program play all night long, even while we're sleeping.

For us, night is supposed to be about "downtime." Health professionals suggest we develop routines that make us sleepy before bedtime—drink something warm, limit artificial light from digital devices, or read a book, for example. These practices help our minds and bodies slow down and move toward a state of nonawareness in sleep.

But while we are down, God is up! The spotlight on His creation is always blazing, day or night. And, if you're having one of those nights when you can't sleep, you can count on its inspiration. Maybe you suffer from insomnia, maybe your latest chemo round is making you sick, maybe you're nursing a newborn, maybe you've recently been widowed. . . . God sees the reason and He beckons you through His light. It could be the moonbeam that splashes through your window, or maybe it's a special insight you gain as you read His Word. His power reaches from the farthest heavens to your own need.

. . . .

Heavenly Father, I love Your creation! Tonight, I'm looking and
listening as You display Your power in the night sky. Amen.

NIGHT LEADING

*And the L*ORD *went before them by day in a pillar of*
cloud to lead the way, and by night in a pillar of fire to
give them light, so as to go by day and night.
EXODUS 13:21 NKJV

Some problems have to be solved at night. While conventional wisdom may argue for morning light and clear heads, some crises cannot wait. And some of us have to be the ones to deal with trouble:

A law enforcement officer bringing control to a crime scene.

A surgeon called into the operating room for a life-saving procedure.

A nurse administering medications at the crucial moment.

A counselor talking to a person contemplating suicide.

A mother cleaning up her sick child's room.

A parent interceding for a rebellious teen somewhere on the streets.

God knew that His people, who were journeying toward the Promised Land, needed guidance at night as well as during the day. It seems that there were times when they had to travel by night. And He made sure they had the means to do that.

Rest was God's intent for our nights on earth. But if you have to be up for some reason, you can know that His power to lead you is not dependent on the rising of the sun. You're in good hands tonight.

. . . .

Father in heaven, lead me as I work tonight.
I'm looking for that pillar of fire. Amen.

THE ARMY IS GATHERING

Therefore he sent horses and chariots and a great army there, and they came by night and surrounded the city.

2 KINGS 6:14 NKJV

I like being surrounded by family or friends—but definitely **not by enemies**. Well, I hope I don't even have enough enemies to make **an army**, but if I did, I wouldn't want them ganging up on me. Especially **at night**!

But that's what happened to God's prophet Elisha in this Old **Testament** story. The king of Syria was determined to rid himself of the prophet **who** could discern his battle plans and was telling the king of Israel. So **he sent** his band of big, bad Syrian soldiers to the city of Dothan, where Elisha **lived**.

Have you ever been in a situation like that? A place in a relationship **or your** own emotions, a place of a financial or health crisis that **felt like** the enemy had you surrounded?

If tonight you feel yourself being smothered by problems, be **strengthened by** the words Elisha said to his servant: "Do not fear, for **those who** are with us are more than those who are with them" (2 Kings **6:16 NKJV**).

God also has an army—a gathering of angels who do **His bidding. And** they still have chariots of fire at their disposal. Go to **sleep knowing that if** you are trusting God, you are better protected than you can even **imagine**.

. . . .

Oh God, give me the faith to rest in Your protection tonight. No army can bring a siege against me that You cannot break. I trust You. Amen.

ORDER AND RITUAL

*Give thanks. . .to him who made the great lights. . .the sun to
rule over the day. . .the moon and stars to rule over the night,
for his steadfast love endures forever.*

PSALM 136:1, 7–9 ESV

My guess is that you brush your teeth every night before you go to bed. It's
part of your nightly ritual. There is an order to what you do.

Most of us owe our mothers for our devotion to this ritual of good
hygiene. Because of their guidance, it's part of the order of our bedtime
routine.

There is also an order to the universe. In fact, orderliness is a trait of
our wonderful Creator. He does not do things haphazardly or at random.
We can see the steady, orderly nature of His character in the night sky. The
moon and stars have been overseeing Earth's nightly rituals for millennia.
They will continue to do so until He replaces the current system with a
better one. In fact, we are also told that in our eternal home, we won't even
need a sun because the Lamb is the light. It goes without saying that we
won't need a moon, a reflector of the sun, either.

For now though, brush your teeth and go to bed. God built the need
for order into us as well, and we can feel secure under the moonbeams
of this orderly Lord.

. . . .

*Creator Father, thank You for the great lights. Keep me
steadfast in You tonight. In Jesus' name, amen.*

NIGHT DUTY

Now these, the singers, the heads of fathers' houses of
the Levites, were in the chambers of the temple free from
other service, for they were on duty day and night.
1 CHRONICLES 9:33 ESV

Most night singers in the twenty-first century work in nightclubs, not churches. But in this ancient record, from the days just following the Israelites' Babylonian exile, the singers were working for the glory of God, not for a tittering, drunken crowd. They had an around-the-clock assignment at the tabernacle. I'm not exactly sure what that meant: Did they have to be ready to sing at any moment of the day or night? Did they minister through the night hours? Was there continual singing in the tabernacle? Whatever the details, these musicians did not shirk from their night duty.

You and I don't have a nightly assignment in the tabernacle, but we are called to around-the-clock faithfulness. Often, in the night hours, temptation seems stronger and willpower weaker. So many sins are committed in the nighttime—as Jesus said in John 3:19, men love darkness because their acts are evil.

But if these Old Testament singers could be on duty for God twenty-four hours a day, so can we—not necessarily for making music, but for living obediently.

. . . .

Lord God, I want to be a faithful, around-the-clock
servant. Thank You for the grace to do it. Amen.

PINCHES AND THROBS

"The night racks my bones, and the pain that gnaws me takes no rest."
JOB 30:17 ESV

Are you hurting tonight as you climb into bed?

Who me? I'm not that old! I don't have arthritis.

Okay, great. But younger women have health issues too. Whether you experience autoimmune diseases like lupus and multiple sclerosis, heart disease or cancer, or just the common monthly throes of being female, there is no shortage of reasons for pain. Some conditions are worse than others, but none of them are pleasant—especially when you're trying to sleep.

Most of us know the story of Job, the godly man of ancient times who went through severe testing. If ever a human knew about suffering of all kinds—relational, emotional, financial, physical, spiritual—Job did. He had pain on every level. And even at night, he got no rest. Job's body was so riddled with the effects of his crises that he found no relief.

Belonging to Christ does not alleviate every bit of suffering. We still live on a cursed and broken planet, and we are still subject to earthly circumstances. But we do know that our Lord experienced the things we go through—and that He has promised never to leave us. That includes our painful nights too, and sometimes just having Someone with us makes things bearable. It did for Job.

. . . .

*Lord, I'm glad You're with me always, even in my pain.
I know I can depend on Your grace and presence. Amen.*

COME AT NIGHT

There was a man of the Pharisees named Nicodemus,
a ruler of the Jews. This man came to Jesus by night.
JOHN 3:1–2 NKJV

One of my favorite books by Dr. Seuss concerns a certain **Marvin K. Mooney**, who is told "the time has come to go, Go, GO!"

In his own inimitable way, Theodore Seuss Geisel fills this **children's book** with all manner of cartoon illustrations of ways that Marvin **can go**. What he is supposed to do *after* he goes, we're not told. But it **seems imperative** that Marvin go—at once!

The biblical Nicodemus must have felt an urgency to go too—**to see Jesus**. We know that Nicodemus was a member of the Jewish **ruling committee**, the Sanhedrin. He was a Pharisee, holding an **important position** in the church and community. But he had a deep need and **he was desperate** to do something about it. He apparently wasn't willing **to be a public** follower of Jesus at this time, but he knew that Jesus had **answers to his questions**.

Do you need to go to Jesus tonight? Do you have a **desperate need in your soul**, your emotions, your family? Don't delay. Go now. He is **waiting for you to draw near**.

. . . .

God, I come to You in Jesus' name and bring my deep need.
Thank You for always being available, even at night. Amen.

DELIVERANCE AT NIGHT

Then the high priest rose up, and all those who were with him (which is the sect of the Sadducees), and they were filled with indignation, and laid their hands on the apostles and put them in the common prison. But at night an angel of the Lord opened the prison doors and brought them out, and said, "Go, stand in the temple and speak to the people all the words of this life."

ACTS 5:17–20 NKJV

I've heard parents say that they like to take road trips at night because the children will sleep most of the way. The drone of the motor and the motion of the vehicle lull little minds and bodies to dreamland. For parents, children sleeping through long trips adds a sweet dimension to vacation.

While moving vehicles make children feel sleepy, I would guess that the steel bars and iron bunks of a jail might make prisoners feel rowdy. In Acts 5, we don't see exactly what the prisoners were doing when the Lord's angel arrived to release the apostles. We just know that God chose the nighttime to perform this miracle.

What kind of deliverance do you need tonight? There are many kinds of prisons, with bars made of substance abuse, pornographic images, overeating, compulsive gambling, and various anxieties. But from every one of these, God stands ready to deliver.

. . . .

Almighty God, I need You to open the door of my prison tonight and lead me out. In Jesus' name, amen.

NO DIFFERENCE

*Indeed, the darkness shall not hide from You, but the night shines
as the day; the darkness and the light are both alike to You.*
PSALM 139:12 NKJV

I've always been intrigued by night-vision goggles. You know, the kind of eyewear the military uses in covert nighttime operations. Soldiers can see in the darkness as people and things take on an eerie greenish glow. But it's not quite like the illumination of actual daylight.

With our God, however, His vision is the same day or night. Because He *is* light, He has no need for any other source. Wherever God is, He can see fully.

God sees all the details on this planet at every moment. He can see the people and the situations, the sins and the sorrows. He sees *you*. The darkness of this night cannot keep Him from noticing everything about you. The fears you're harboring (and maybe feeling silly about)—He sees, and He cares. The guilt that threatens to swallow you—He sees, and He forgives. The longings in your heart that no one has ever really understood—He sees, and He loves.

Don't try to hide from God—you can't do that anyway. His light can warm your soul and bring out the beauty He's placed inside you.

. . . .

*Father God, You see me right now, not as a dim shadow,
but in living color and 3-D high definition. I invite You
to shine Your light on me. In Jesus' name, amen.*

THE TRUST OF OBLIVION

But as for me, I trust in You, O LORD; I say,
"You are my God." My times are in Your hand.
PSALM 31:14–15 NKJV

I read somewhere that being willing to lie down at night and go to sleep evidences our trust in God—not only trust that we will be safe but also trust that He can run the world without us. We're admitting that He can manage things while we sleep.

That's both convicting and reassuring. Maybe it's because I'm a firstborn that I think I need to be aware of the plan and all the details in order for everything to come out okay. I really like information. In fact, I have trouble warding off anxiety if I don't know how things are going. This can be irritating to other people, and I'm sure the Lord doesn't really want me quizzing *Him* about what He is doing!

So it makes a lot of sense to say, "Okay, Lord, I'm going to sleep now. I know You've got things here. I'm human and need sleep. You're divine and don't. I'm trusting You to keep everything going while I rest." Kind of freeing, huh? Being willing to surrender our minds and bodies to the oblivion of sleep is a declaration of trust that we can make every night.

. . . .

Father in heaven, my days and nights, my times, are Yours. Tonight, I trust
You with the world—and my world in particular—while I sleep. Amen.

SMARTER IN THE MORNING

I will bless the Lord who counsels me; he gives me
wisdom in the night. He tells me what to do.
PSALM 16:7 TLB

Have you ever gone to bed with a problem that had no **answer and awakened with** an idea of what to do?

Your experience is not uncommon. Research has shown that **the subconscious** mind is always working, even when we sleep. We may be **zoned out** in la-la land, but the magnificent brain God gave us is still on **the job.** Sometimes, the solution to the problem was there all the time—our **mind** just needed to quiet down and find it!

God made us, so of course He understands this reality. He **designed sleep for** many reasons, and this may well be one of them. If we are **in a close and** growing relationship with Him, we'll always have the **counsel of** His Word and His Spirit—and oftentimes He'll speak to us in the **twilight of our** consciousness, before we drift off to sleep, or in that early **morning haze as** we begin to awaken.

Your dilemma may seem unsolvable tonight, but don't **get worked up** about it. Give your mind **a chance** to rest—and God a **chance to show you** something you haven't thought about yet. You'll be smarter in the morning.

. . . .

Father, I need guidance and direction. I need a solution.
Give me Your wisdom. Open my understanding so that when
I awaken, I will know what to do. In Jesus' name, amen.

GET YOUR BEAUTY SLEEP

My sleep was sweet unto me.
JEREMIAH 31:26 KJV

It's what we say when we need an excuse to go to bed: "Well, I need to get my beauty sleep."

That could be interpreted in a couple of ways. We're either humbly saying, "I won't even look presentable if I don't sleep," or vainly boasting, "You know, I have to preserve this good thing I've got going."

It is true that a part of healthy self-care is getting rest. The body does show the effects of sleep deprivation, with dark circles and bags under the eyes, complexion issues, heightened effects of aging, and on and on. So sleep is a good idea to care for the womanly beauty God has given us.

The context of this verse from the Old Testament, though, is not beauty sleep. It was the prophet Jeremiah's assurances from the Lord about the future of Israel. Because of that, he considered the night of sleep he had just enjoyed as very sweet.

You and I need reassurance from the Lord about our futures too, and He has given us many promises—both for our lives on earth and in eternity. They will make the sleep we get even more effective, for we can truly relax and gain the benefit for both our bodies and minds.

. . . .

*God, tonight give me rest and reassurance. Thank You for
the womanly beauty You've given me. Help me to steward it
appropriately by getting rest tonight. In Jesus' name, amen.*

WHEN JESUS SLEEPS

*And suddenly a great tempest arose on the sea, so that the
boat was covered with the waves. But He was asleep.*
MATTHEW 8:24 NKJV

We know He slept.

Jesus was fully human as well as fully divine. He had a **human body
like ours** that required food and rest. He must have been tired **often in
the** demands of His public ministry. But the only record we have **of Him
sleeping** is during a storm.

Many details of Jesus' life on earth are not given to us. Surely His **disciples** observed Him sleeping at other times, but that wasn't something **God
inspired** them to write down. We know about it in this context **because
it was** important to the narrative: Jesus was, get this, *sleeping* **during a
violent** storm on the water.

In His earthly body, Jesus needed sleep. Though He was God **on earth
and had** an eternal mission to accomplish, He realized His human **limitations and** succumbed to His need of rest.

If Jesus needed that, we need it too. I don't have to tell **you that we don't
have the awesome mission He had**—but there is some **mission for each one
of us**. To fulfill it, we'll have to sleep once in a while. Maybe even in a storm.

. . . .

*Lord Jesus, thank You for giving us a good example in everything,
even in getting sleep. I'm going to get my eight hours now. Amen.*

SLEEPING YOURSELF POOR

*Love not sleep, lest you come to poverty; open your
eyes, and you will have plenty of bread.*
PROVERBS 20:13 ESV

Yeah, I know these devotionals are supposed to be encouraging. What's with this talk about being poor if you sleep?

Well, there is a balance here. We need to keep sleep in proper perspective.

I've already confessed that I don't always appreciate sleep. So I lean toward one side of the scales. But, because of the various human temperaments, there are others who see sleep as a pleasure—and have a difficult time limiting that indulgence. Both perspectives are skewed and detrimental to the lives God wants us to lead.

The writer of Proverbs warns his readers about *loving* sleep. Maybe we should develop a similar attitude as the one we have toward food: it's necessary for the body, pleasant, and to be enjoyed at the right time. But it cannot be the focus of living.

Of course, there are seasons of life when getting sleep is more challenging or more necessary. New babies, health issues, caregiving for the chronically ill—all of these circumstances can tweak our sleep cycles. We need to be realistic about that. But, in general, let's heed the Word and keep sleep in its proper place. If not, you might just find yourself not only sleepy, but poor to boot.

. . . .

*Lord, thank You for helping me keep balance through
the truth of Your Word. Tonight, I embrace sleep at the
right time and for the right reasons. Amen.*

WAKE UP!

So then let us not sleep, as others do, but let us keep awake and be sober.
For those who sleep, sleep at night, and those who get drunk, are drunk
at night. But since we belong to the day, let us be sober, having put on
the breastplate of faith and love, and for a helmet the hope of salvation.
1 THESSALONIANS 5:6–8 ESV

If it's important to keep our desire for sleep in proper perspective, it is likewise vital to know when to wake up!

My natural body rhythm is to stay up late and then sleep through morning. But as I have tried to reset my body and get up earlier, I've discovered a cool thing—mornings are pretty great. Seeing the golden haze of an early morning and feeling anticipation as the mist rolls off the fields is actually very inspiring. I'm still not really a morning person, but I sure am appreciating morning a lot more.

God uses the physical world to teach spiritual truths. Through the apostle Paul, the Lord tells us not to be lethargic and sleepy in a spiritual sense, but rather to know when to be awake and alert. Our physical bodies must be engaged while it is day, and our spiritual selves should be as well.

. . . .

Father, You have made me to be alert in the daylight hours. Let me
also be aware spiritually and not be fooled by Satan's plans. Amen.

INTERRUPTED SLEEP

For you yourselves are fully aware that the day of
the Lord will come like a thief in the night.

1 THESSALONIANS 5:2 ESV

My husband is a light sleeper and does not like his sleep to be interrupted. But because he awakens easily, my nocturnal habits often cause him grief. No matter how quiet I try to be, he always seems to wake up. My creeping about and trying to open doors silently are in vain.

In today's scripture, we are given a bit of wonderful imagery: "the *day* of the Lord will come like a thief in the *night*." I believe that contrast is purposeful. The light of Jesus' coming will shine in eternal glory and purity against the twisted and polluted backdrop of this world, where Satan is the prince of the power of the air. Jesus' arrival will bring to a halt all the sleepiness of a world oblivious to the heavenly kingdom. The time for nonchalance will be over. Judgment will come.

To those in relationship with Him, the coming of Jesus will not be a troubling interruption but a welcomed event. He is not coming as a thief to those who look for Him. No, they anticipate His coming like a bride awaits her wedding day—with joy and longing.

. . . .

Lord Jesus, I wait for Your coming with joy so that I
can be with You always. If you come tonight while I
sleep, I will wake up in Your presence. Amen.

SLEEP LIKE A BABY

You will keep him in perfect peace, whose mind is
stayed on You, because he trusts in You.
ISAIAH 26:3 NKJV

You've heard the expression, "I slept like a baby last night." Probably used it yourself.

We say this to describe a period of restful, unbroken sleep from which we awaken refreshed. But it's probable that babies don't always sleep as well as we think, right? I'm sure they have dreams and times of restlessness when they don't feel comfortable—they just don't have the self-awareness to understand it or the ability to describe it. But, exceptions notwithstanding, the phrase has come to describe the kind of sleep we all want when we pull back the covers at night.

The prophet Isaiah says that a restful mind is possible if we keep our thoughts centered on God. That makes sense in the daytime, when we're actively using our minds. But even though we may not be able to control our dreams, before we sleep we can focus our thoughts on the One who controls our universe and everything in it.

The Hebrew wording of this verse seems to imply that the person whose mind is centered on God will have "peace upon peace"—peace in abundance, both now and forever. That sounds like an amazing sleep aid. I'm going to try it tonight. How about you?

. . . .

God, I turn my thoughts to You tonight. Keep me and
give me peace upon peace. In Jesus' name, amen.

Section 2:
NEXT DAY

TOMORROW

"Therefore do not be anxious about tomorrow, for tomorrow will be anxious for itself. Sufficient for the day is its own trouble."
MATTHEW 6:34 ESV

Annie, the little orphan girl with red hair, sang about how she loved "tomorrow." The classic ending phrase of the chorus says tomorrow is "only a day away."

Children seem to feel the anticipation of tomorrow; adults not so much. As we get older, take on more responsibilities, and understand the complications of life in succeeding seasons, many of us tend more toward apprehension.

But Jesus said an emphatic "no" to this approach. In His wonderful Sermon on the Mount, He told those gathered on a Judean hillside (and us sitting on our beds tonight) that we should not be anxious about tomorrow. We must purposely fight anxiety by reminding ourselves of the truth: we can't live tomorrow yet, and God will be there when it arrives.

This is easy to say and difficult to do. But tonight, as you get ready to sleep, open your heart to a tiny ray of anticipation. Tomorrow might be beautiful, ordinary, or shocking. But whatever comes, it's going to be all right. . .because God will be there too!

. . . .

Heavenly Father, I release into Your hands my anxiety about tomorrow. Help me look forward to spending the day with You. In Jesus' name, amen.

TOMORROW WITH THEM

Bearing with one another, and forgiving one another, if anyone has a complaint against another; even as Christ forgave you, so you also must do. But above all these things put on love, which is the bond of perfection.
COLOSSIANS 3:13–14 NKJV

Family is forever. Well, in a manner of speaking. Of course, if we know Jesus, we will be family for eternity, and that's super cool. But generally when people use this phrase, they mean that no matter what happens, you're connected to your origins. You may have irritating uncles, gushy aunts, bratty cousins, bossy sisters, hovering parents, and the like, but they'll always be part of where you came from—and usually connected to your future.

Tomorrow, you will probably have some kind of interaction with your family. Young or old; single, married, or widowed; parent or childless, nearly everyone will have a contact with family, either in a house or by phone, text, or social media.

You may have a negative track record with your family. Yours may be positive. Either way, tomorrow is another day, full of possibilities. God calls us in Colossians 3 to forbearance and forgiveness and love—which according to Him completes the loop in every relationship.

. . . .

Heavenly Father, You have given me the promise of tomorrow, and I ask You to help me use it in good ways with my family. Amen.

THE TO-DO LIST FOR TOMORROW

A man's heart plans his way, but the LORD directs his steps.
PROVERBS 16:9 NKJV

I have a love-hate relationship with to-do lists.

I have often gone to bed at night dreading the next morning. Why? Because of the laundry list of chores and responsibilities hanging over my head. And sometimes I arise in the morning with the same unpleasant outlook. I'm sure that's *not* what God intended when He instituted the sleep cycle for us. I feel confident that He wants us to have goals and an orderly life. But He does not want us to be slaves to some compulsive idea of "order." God wants balance for us, and lists can be part of that balance—if we use them sensibly. The writer of Proverbs says that God is the One who ultimately directs our steps.

Maybe, like me, you're a list maker. If so, let's do our best to be reasonable when we chalk out our plans for the coming day—no week's worth of duties in a twenty-four-hour period, please. And let's use our lists as tools for our good. When they cease to be helpful, let's try something else, okay?

. . . .

Lord, thank You for creating a world of order. Bless my to-do list for tomorrow. Let me glorify You in what I accomplish. Amen.

FIRST THIS, THEN THAT

*"For it is precept upon precept, precept upon precept,
line upon line, line upon line, here a little, there a little."*
ISAIAH 28:10 ESV

I'm a sequential kind of person. I tend to pull back from the mishmash, isolating a single thread to work on before going to the next. When my children struggle with a list of overwhelming tasks, I often remind them of this homely wisdom: "You eat the elephant one bite at a time!"

I've discovered that if I step back, take a breath, and identify the most pressing responsibility, I can make progress and eventually conquer the monster.

How about you? Maybe you're of a different temperament. Maybe the pressure of multiple tasks threatens to smother you. None of us sleep well when we feel like we're under intense pressure.

Today's scripture, from the book of Isaiah, reminds us that we must advance by degrees, little by little. This works both in the spiritual realm and in the mundane duties of everyday life.

Tonight, as you try to fall asleep, remind yourself that you *can* accomplish and conquer tomorrow. Just approach your job with a "first this, then that" attitude. You go, girl!

. . . .

*God, I plan to approach tomorrow with the promise of Your
strength as I conquer my duties, one bite at a time. Amen.*

THAT NEEDED GAP

"The whole earth is at rest and quiet."
ISAIAH 14:7 NKJV

Some of us would fuse one day right into the next, right?

There are so many things on our bucket lists and so many dragons to slay and roses to smell that we would do away with sleep if it were physically possible. But God knew that wouldn't be good for us. He created the night hours to be a buffer, a gap between our battle zones.

Health professionals and business management executives recognize that minds and bodies can't go nonstop at full capacity. But they weren't the first ones to know that—God had it figured out from the beginning. In fact, He set in place the laws that govern our bodies and the universe. From the first day of creation, He planned for there to be a gap between daylight hours—a gap called night.

Today's verse, from Isaiah, describes a world at peace after the fall of Babylon's king. But it's a nice way to describe what God intended nighttime to be—a tranquil space of rest for everyone. That's not always a reality, but we must still recognize and embrace the idea that night is a needed buffer for us. We operate best when we have this cushion between the busyness of our days.

Don't fight the night gap. Make it work for you so you can be ready for tomorrow!

. . . .

Father in heaven, You are Lord of the night as well as the day. Thank You for this needed gap of inactivity. Amen.

RACE TO MORNING

For all our days are passed away in thy wrath:
we spend our years as a tale that is told.
PSALM 90:9 KJV

Does your nighttime seem to be a race to the morning?

Mornings can be a mixed bag, shaped by the expectations of jobs and our family dynamic. At one time in my life, to get to the private school my children attended and then to my job, I had an hour-long commute. Since some of it took place in the city (and during the winter those northeastern Ohio roads could be difficult), mornings were often a stressful period of the day. And the way life goes, it seemed like I was always back in the van, making that coffee-fueled commute, all too quickly the next day.

The psalmist wrote that our days pass quickly, and our years are like a tale that has already been told. Some mornings go by so fast that we can't even remember how the story began! Thankfully, not all of them are like that—and even when they are, God has given us time for rest and recuperation.

As you get into bed tonight, try to change your thinking about the coming morning. After all, night isn't a time to race but to rest.

. . . .

Lord, let me leave the race to morning with You.
However long the night seems, it is Yours too. Amen.

MAKE YOUR COFFEE

She gets up before dawn to prepare breakfast for her
household and plans the day's work for her servant girls.
PROVERBS 31:15 TLB

No, coffee isn't mentioned in the Bible.

This verse, from the life of the famous "Proverbs 31 Woman," doesn't have anything to say about coffee, only breakfast in general. Coffee seems to have originated in the Middle East or possibly on the African continent, much later than Bible times. But we know how important it is to us in our culture.

If you have the old drip-brewer, perhaps you do what I used to—the night before, you insert a new filter, add the grounds, fill the reservoir, and set the timer, so when you get up, hot coffee awaits you. If you have a more modern machine, you might select the single-serve cup you want, check the water level, and set out either a cup or a travel mug for the next day. Either way, prep the night before saves time in the morning, getting you more quickly to that fragrant aroma and longed-for flavor as you emerge from your bedroom.

So why are you still sitting here reading, girlfriend? Go get your morning prep done. And then get in bed. Tomorrow is coming.

· ·

Lord, thank You for coffee, tea, fruit juice, diet soda—the liquids
that fuel our mornings. You give us many simple pleasures in life,
and I'm looking forward to my cup in the morning. Amen.

RISE AND SHINE

Arise, shine; for your light has come! And the
glory of the LORD is risen upon you.
ISAIAH 60:1 NKJV

My mother used to say it to me: "Rise and shine!" And in typical kid fashion, I probably groaned. Bed and warm blankets seemed much more glorious than getting up to shine.

Some people bounce out of bed in the morning with a song for the world; these women flick on the lights, throw open the windows, and start frying bacon. Others of us ease out of bed, not saying much until after we've been up for a little while. We turn on a soft lamp, crack open the blinds, and stir up some oatmeal. For us, the idea of blinding the world with a brilliant smile the first thing in the morning is almost unbearable—we need to be "gentled" into the day as the light arrives.

There's another light, though—the Light of the World—that arose at the coming of Jesus and still shines on us all. I wonder if Mom's saying came from this verse. Back then, I sure never thought she was quoting scripture to me on those school mornings!

Anyway, go to sleep tonight with the knowledge that Jesus has come and His light shines for you—whether you bounce or shuffle in the morning.

. . . .

Heavenly Father, I'm glad Your light shines all day and
all night too. I need Your glory in my life, and I ask You
to shine on me tomorrow. In Jesus' name, amen.

LOOK FOR DELIGHT

"For you shall go out with joy, and be led out with peace;
the mountains and the hills shall break forth into singing before
you, and all the trees of the field shall clap their hands."
ISAIAH 55:12 NKJV

It's certainly not a universal feeling, but for some of us, bedtime can be a downer.

As shadows fall and the night sounds begin, people with a streak of melancholy can slide into moodiness. With the day's activities winding down and the world going inside for the night, some can forget that tomorrow, once again, the sun will shine and the birds will chirp, the stores will open and life will resume its busy routine.

Our heavenly Father wants us to anticipate each day with joy. The prophet promised his nation that a day was coming when even nature itself would sing and applaud. God makes those days of celebration and victory and joy possible. Who knows? Tomorrow could be one of them!

Tonight's emotions do not determine how tomorrow will go. But they can certainly affect your attitude as you go to sleep. Give God credit: He can handle tomorrow. Look forward with delight.

. . . .

Oh God, You are the eternal Being of joy. Tonight, I look ahead to
tomorrow and determine to find every bit of delight You give to me. Amen.

THE ADVENTURE AWAITS

This is the day the LORD has made; we will rejoice and be glad in it.
PSALM 118:24 NKJV

If you grew up in the church, no doubt you've been singing this little chorus since your days in Sunday school: "This is the day (this is the day), that the Lord hath made (that the Lord hath made). . . ." We could sing it in our sleep. But do we really embrace its message?

Life is made up of days and nights, one upon the other. They're segments of a grand adventure the Master Storyteller is writing for us. He knows that every single day is important to the plot. He sees the glorious ending and is working to bring all the pieces of the narrative together in a wonderful way. One day, in eternity, we might look back at the story of our lives and be amazed—far more than we are with the skill of a favorite novelist or screenwriter now.

The writer of this psalm invites us to rejoice in the day the Creator has given us. And we'll include the anticipation of *tomorrow* in that joy! God has planned an adventure for you. Now go to sleep. It won't be long until the next chapter begins.

. . . .

Father God, thank You for writing my story. I know
You have the plot well laid out. I'm looking forward to
what happens tomorrow. In Jesus' name, amen.

HAVE A BLESSED DAY

Blessed be the Lord, who daily bears us up; God is our salvation.
PSALM 68:19 ESV

It's become a common phrase. Some people leave it on their voice mail greeting. Even store clerks might say the words: "Have a blessed day."

The words are more common to people of faith, but I suppose even unbelievers occasionally use them. (I do wonder whom they think is doing the blessing.) But it's a nice, cheerful thing to say and a pleasant alternative to the perennial "Enjoy your day!" A person using the phrase is trying to wish another well—to give "good vibes," some might say. But there is a spiritual truth behind these words.

God really does bless our days. In fact, this verse from Psalm 68 tells us that He "bears us up" every day. The original language indicates something like, "He helps us bear our daily load." That kind of help can bless anybody's day, wouldn't you agree?

It's bedtime now. Today is almost over, but tomorrow lies ahead. And the God who bore you up today will do the same tomorrow. He never changes His ideas about grace. He is near to all who call on Him in truth. Those are pretty good thoughts to go to bed on.

. . . .

Father in heaven, You helped me bear up today. Thank You.
I couldn't have done it without Your grace. Tomorrow too
I know You will help me. I praise You for it. Amen.

WHERE MORNING BEGINS

Your people will offer themselves willingly in the day of Your power, in the beauty of holiness and in holy array out of the womb of the morning.

PSALM 110:3 AMPC

We women are well acquainted with the importance of the womb. It's the cocoon for babies, the sacred and secret place where embryonic life is nurtured and prepared for the outside world. Ask a newly expectant mother who thrills to every imagined twinge within her. Talk to the woman about to deliver, for whom the daily jabs and twistings of the child inside have become like an acrobatics show. Inquire with the surgeon who enters this hallowed chamber to perform procedures on tiny organs and limbs. They'll tell you: the uterus, the womb, is a place of wonders. It cradles the beginnings of life.

The psalmist David declared that morning has a womb. Where would that be? In the blackness before dawn, in the first streaks of pink and gold, in the east where the sun rises? Let's suppose that the "womb of the morning" is the night before. Imagine that bedtime is a sacred ritual and sleep a holy state in which you are nurtured and prepared for the coming day.

. . . .

Father, You made the human womb and You made the morning's womb. Both denote life and joy. I rest now in the knowledge that You will birth the new day for my benefit. Amen.

WHAT YOU WILL CREATE

In the morning sow your seed, and at evening withhold
not your hand, for you do not know which will prosper,
this or that, or whether both alike will be good.

ECCLESIASTES 11:6 ESV

Are you thinking tonight about what you have to do tomorrow?

Are you wondering how you will get it all done? Are you **pondering** if you should even try? Are you wishing you had another job, **another** assignment, another calling, another life?

We've all experienced those emotions. Our enemy, Satan, makes **cer-**tain that we're aware of all those other people who seem to have **more** glamorous and fulfilling lives. When it comes to his agenda with **women,** he specializes in comparison.

God calls to you tonight with a different message. He tells you **to get** up in the morning to do your work, and then to stay busy in the **evening** too. Were you born to paint or design or sculpt or garden? Do you **excel in** baking or making soap or refinishing old furniture? Go at your **day—your** vocation and your avocation—with zest and hope. Refuse to **give up. And** somewhere between responsibility and creativity you may **just find the** sweet spot for which He made you.

. . . .

God, I ask You to show me how to find joy in what I do tomorrow.
Help me balance both the necessary tasks and my internal longings
to create. I embrace the woman You made in me. Amen.

PLAN NOW

Direct my steps by Your word, and let no iniquity have dominion over me.
PSALM 119:133 NKJV

"What are you doing today?"

God really doesn't need to ask us what we're doing tomorrow. He already knows what that will be. But He does like to hear from us, and He wants to help us with our planning.

The psalmist prayed that the Lord would direct his steps. That should be our prayer too. When we ask God about our plans for tomorrow, we have the benefit of His wisdom and the knowledge that He is part of all we do.

Making plans the night before can help us to rest easier. Plotting out the next day makes our morning less vague. I believe it even allows our subconscious mind to work on the details ahead of time!

Take a moment to ask God about your tomorrow. Make a note—either mentally or on a piece of paper if you're feeling energetic—of what you need to accomplish. Don't forget to schedule some downtime. Then thank God for His guidance and lay down to your rest. You're going to do amazing things tomorrow!

. . . .

*Father, I bring my plans to You. Direct me and give
me energy and joy. In Jesus' name, amen.*

DAWN'S RISING

*[The crocodile's] sneezings flash forth light, and his
eyes are like the [reddish] eyelids of the dawn.*
JOB 41:18 AMPC

The ancient Egyptian hieroglyph for morning is the crocodile's eyes.
Because they emerge from the water before the rest of the animal's head
and body, a long-ago artist chose them to represent dawn.

It's certainly not a comforting image for early morning, is it? For those
like me who prefer "gentle awakenings," it's almost revolting. But it's easy
to grasp the connection. And with the Nile River most assuredly full of
crocodiles, nearly every ancient Egyptian understood it immediately.

What is your symbol for morning? An alarm clock? A coffee mug? A
day planner?

Consider how you could envision morning more positively in your
mind. It just might change your attitude a bit, helping you focus on the
fresh opportunities ahead.

I'll never see a crocodile's eyes again without thinking of those Egyptians
and their morning symbol. But that only reminds me of a bigger, better
reality: the dawn belongs to God, and His eyes are always open.

. . . .

*Lord, You made the morning and You made me.
Tonight, as I go to sleep, help me picture morning as the
fabulous time of day You meant it to be. Amen.*

ALWAYS HOPE

But I will hope continually, and will praise You yet more and more.

There are few things worse than hopelessness.

Maybe you find yourself in that situation tonight. Or at least it seems to be your situation. But that's a lie from the enemy. Because of Christ, there is always hope—hope for tonight and its troubles, hope for tomorrow and its needs.

When I worked as a volunteer counselor at a faith-based pregnancy center, I saw women who thought they had no hope. Some were pregnant and didn't want to be, some were living a promiscuous lifestyle and feeling guilt, and some were post-abortive and sure they were unforgivable. I had the awesome privilege to tell them that there *was* hope—for the present because of the resources we offered but also for the future (all eternity, really) because of Christ.

I give you the same message tonight.

Whatever your addictions.

Whatever your messed-up life.

Whatever your failures.

Whatever your rebellion.

Whatever your track record.

You have hope, continually, because of Jesus. If you simply ask, you can rest tonight in His mercy. And you can anticipate tomorrow because of His grace.

. . . .

Father God, tonight I bring my hopelessness to You and ask to exchange it for Your rest and peace. In Jesus' name, amen.

CONQUERORS UNLIMITED

Yet in all these things we are more than
conquerors through Him who loved us.
ROMANS 8:37 NKJV

First-century Christians knew a lot about conquerors. They lived in Rome, the dominant power of the world. They had seen the gladiators and witnessed fights to the death. Soldiers were part of the daily scene. Rome was a nation of conquerors.

In recent years, Christian musicians and speakers have emphasized the idea of overcoming. It's a message we all need and want to hear. And it's based in the truth of God's Word.

The apostle Paul, writer of Romans, listed all kinds of catastrophes and asked if any of them could separate us from the love of Christ. The answer— *no!* And then Paul shared this verse to show that we can conquer anything because of the One whose love redeemed us.

What do you need to conquer tomorrow? What is clogging your mind tonight as you try to drift off to sleep?

There are medications to help us fall asleep, but there are no chemicals that can do what God's love can—make us "more than conquerors." Embrace the power of Jesus tonight.

. . . .

Heavenly Father, thank You for the power to overcome through
Your Son. As I think about my day tomorrow, I ask You to give me
strength to battle my way through anything that stands in the
way of fulfilling Your purpose in me. In Jesus' name, amen.

OPEN HANDS

Let my prayer be counted as incense before you, and the lifting up of my hands as the evening sacrifice!
PSALM 141:2 ESV

What do you do with your hands while you sleep?

Babies usually sleep with hands made into tiny fists. Perhaps this is because of the startle reflex we can observe in them. They feel more secure with their hands tightly closed.

I think adults have an inclination to do the same, in a figurative sense. Most of us are keenly aware of the possibility of loss—and we want to do everything we can to keep that from happening. We want to control the circumstances around us, to try to ward off any potential crisis. That's certainly a natural response.

But our God asks us to trust Him with the control of our lives. The psalm writer calls us to worship God with upraised hands. When we lift our hands in worship, we have to open them—to raise a fist toward the heavens is a gesture of rebellion. But to raise our open hands, palms upward, is to acknowledge that God is the Giver and we are the receivers.

The psalmist's prayer is that his raised hands would be as sacred as the offering of a sacrifice in the evening. Tonight, let's make that our prayer as well.

. . . .

Lord, I lift my hands to You as my offering tonight. May my tomorrow be held in Your control. Amen.

EAT YOUR BREAKFAST

So [Elijah] went and did according to the word of the Lord, for he
went and stayed by the Brook Cherith, which flows into the Jordan.
The ravens brought him bread and meat in the morning, and
bread and meat in the evening; and he drank from the brook.
1 Kings 17:5–6 nkjv

Most of us know that the English word *breakfast* comes from the idea of "breaking the fast" of the night. It's the first meal of the day, the one that fuels our bodies after a period of inactivity and rest. We've also heard the urgings of our mothers and doctors to eat a healthy breakfast. They say it's the most vital meal of the day.

The prophet Elijah had a very unusual breakfast delivery service—ravens. God used His animal creation to help a human being. These birds brought the prophet bread and meat in the morning, as well as the evening.

Elijah's breakfast routine was unique in human history. But breakfast itself is important to everyone. I can tell you that anticipating something delicious and healthy in the morning will make going to sleep a little sweeter. Try it!

. . . .

God, You always find a way to feed Your people. Thank You for the food I
have in my kitchen. I look forward to eating breakfast tomorrow. Amen.

A MORNING PETITION

*But I, O Lord, cry to you; in the
morning my prayer comes before you.*
PSALM 88:13 ESV

If you're a mom (or you've been around babies), you **know the sound that usually** wakes you up in the morning: crying.

That's the only way infants have to call attention to their needs. **It's true that they** sometimes cry just because they're bored or irritable. But **in the morning,** if they're wet or hungry or lonely, they cry. Lying in their **cribs or standing** up if they're older, children wail until Mom or Dad **comes to their** rescue. Soon they learn to smile when they see that familiar **face—it means** relief is coming.

The psalm writer says that he will cry to the Lord. It's a different **cry than a** baby's, but still a heartfelt acknowledgment that he needs the **help of another** for his needs. And in the morning, that kind of petition **is what we need** to speak to God.

In the beginning of this section, we've been discussing the **"next day."** Knowing that we can talk to our Father in heaven when **we awaken the next day brings** comfort **as we go** to bed tonight. Just **as a baby needs** the reassurance of Father or Mother's nearness and help, we need God's presence and grace.

. . . .

*Father in heaven, I'm so glad that You hear my voice when I call
out to You. In the morning, I will be talking to You! Amen.*

SUNRISE, SUNSET

From the rising of the sun to its going down
the LORD's name is to be praised.
PSALM 113:3 NKJV

It's an iconic tune, plaintive in its appeal and simple in its melody. It speaks to the passing years of children's growth—one sunrise and sunset upon another. From a Broadway musical, "Sunrise, Sunset," by Jerry Bock and Sheldon Harnick, became a popular hit.

But long before these men tried to capture the emotion of a father at his daughter's wedding, ancient Hebrew lyricist used the phrase to remind others to praise the name of the Lord—any time of day or night.

Many things can change the way our days play out, but we usually have a consistent time to rise and retire. The psalm writer used these two bookends of the day to illustrate that any time is perfect for praising our God.

As you think about tomorrow, there will be things you know (like the route you take to work or the weather forecast) and things you don't (like the attitudes of your coworkers or the challenges your spouse might face). In the midst of everything, cement in your mind this idea of praising the Lord from sunrise to sunset. It will set a great tone for the entire day.

. . . .

Father God, I praise You tonight as I lay down to sleep.
And I will praise You in the morning when I rise. Amen.

NIGHT FEARS

*He shall cover you with His feathers, and under His wings
you shall take refuge; His truth shall be your shield and
buckler. You shall not be afraid of the terror by night.*
PSALM 91:4–5 NKJV

Thump! Bump! Creak!

Noises in the night sound so loud, don't they? And they're even more frightening when you're alone. It must be the absence of light that makes things in the dark so terrifying. Really, everything else is the same.

But there's a different kind of fear that can be just as scary: fear of night itself.

Some of us just don't like the atmosphere of nighttime. We sense a mood coming over the earth as stores turn off their lights and owls begin to hoot and—in some places—wolves start to howl.

But God, who made the night and understands why we fear it now that sin has warped our world, gives us a promise in the beloved words of Psalm 91. He says we don't have to be afraid of the "terror by night."

Because we're members of God's family, He covers us and gives us refuge. And that means we'll be all right until the morning.

. . . .

*Father, be my shield tonight. Protect me from my fears,
and bring me into the light of morning. In Jesus' name, amen.*

WEAR SOMETHING AMAZING

"Therefore do not be anxious, saying, 'What shall we eat?'
or 'What shall we drink?' or 'What shall we wear?'...
your heavenly Father knows that you need them all."
MATTHEW 6:31–32 ESV

There are very few women who don't think about what they're going to wear. Unless you wear a uniform each day, or are in such dire straits that you have only one outfit, most women will give some thought to what they'll put on each day. Some lay out their clothes the night before; others simply decide in the closet the next morning. But what we wear is a daily consideration.

Evidently, those in Jesus' day were anxious too—not about clothing options, but about clothing in general! He told them (and us) not to be like the pagans who worry about food and drink and clothing, but rather to trust the Father who knows that we need these things.

As you think about the outfit you'll put together for tomorrow (or if you're a mom, wondering if there will even be anything clean to wear), remind yourself that God is fully able to supply what you need. That's a promise from Jesus Himself.

. . . .

Lord God, You have promised to provide what I need. Give me the wisdom
to manage my wardrobe well so that tomorrow I may glorify You. Amen.

SONG FOR MORNING

But I will sing of your strength; I will sing aloud of your
steadfast love in the morning. For you have been to me
a fortress and a refuge in the day of my distress.

PSALM 59:16 ESV

Do you have a morning playlist?

You know what I mean. Most online music sites will let you form playlists of your favorites. One of them ought to be labeled "Morning Music," and jam-packed with songs that motivate and inspire you to be like Jesus. They should be upbeat and positive, pointing you to the truths of God's Word as your strength for the day.

They didn't have Spotify when David penned this psalm—all music was performed live. Maybe some musicians kept their instruments close at hand, to herald the new day with a tune. But however people manage their music—whether it's strummed on a lyre or played from a digital device—we all serve the same God. And He should be the focus of every morning song.

Your mornings might go better if the praise music is already prepared and ready to go. Or you could set your alarm to start with good inspirational Christian music. Let's join David and "sing aloud" of God's steadfast love in the morning!

. . . .

Lord of music, thank You for inspiring men and women who
love You to write down wonderful lyrics for me to use in
worship. I will praise You with my morning song. Amen.

THE OTHER SIDE

The Mighty One, God the LORD, has spoken and called
the earth from the rising of the sun to its going down.
PSALM 50:1 NKJV

Somewhere, it's already tomorrow.

Really—on the other side of the world, it's a completely different time of day. God has arranged this earth on its axis so that its rotation sends the continents through alternating periods of light and darkness. It was part of His good plan.

This little thought bears special significance as we consider the fact of morning. In order for the sun to rise here, it must set somewhere else. And for the opposite side of the world to have a time to rest in the darkness, the sun must blaze down upon us. It's a cycle that God knew would work best for His purposes.

Tonight, comfort yourself with the idea that it's always light somewhere. There is not a speck of land on this planet that is not governed by the Master Creator who declared how all this would work. And He's the One we can call on tonight.

. . . .

Creator God, thank You for Your magnificent plan. Somewhere
right now, while I get ready to sleep, another woman is getting
up to start her day. Bless us both, Lord. In Jesus' name, amen.

Section 3:
SLEEP AIDS

HE IS BIG

Thus says the LORD, your Redeemer, who formed you from the womb: "I am the LORD, who made all things, who alone stretched out the heavens, who spread out the earth by myself."

ISAIAH 44:24 ESV

There's an old gospel song that asks, "How big is God?"

Isaiah answers that question pretty easily. He's big enough to stretch out the heavens and spread out the earth—all by Himself. Though there was a time when the wisest heads of Earth thought that our planet must be flat (and feared that ships could sail too far and fall off the edge of it), today we know our world is round, with a circumference of about 24,900 miles. And God needed no help when He created the earth for us. He's that big.

In fact, God is big enough to cause our planet to revolve around the sun He created, 93 million miles from here. And the universe is exponentially larger than even that distance.

These facts should lead us to restful sleep—because we know that God is big enough for any situation that comes at us. If He can create the very dirt we're standing on, He can take care of any problem that happens on that dirt.

The God who designed this Earth is present with us tonight. Now you should be able to sleep well!

. . . .

Lord of heaven and Earth, thank You for Your magnificent creation of the world, which proves just how majestic You are. Amen.

HE IS SOVEREIGN

For You, LORD, are most high above all the earth;
You are exalted far above all gods.
PSALM 97:9 NKJV

When I was a little girl, my dad was the sovereign in my life. At least in my mind. He was the biggest, most wonderful being I knew. I trusted him. I felt safe when he was around. I knew that he was in control of the things going on around us.

To be sovereign is to be supreme. A sovereign is the one to whom everything belongs and to whom all owe allegiance.

What is sovereign in your life?

Who is sovereign in your life?

When it comes to our feelings of security and peace, especially as nighttime anxieties creep up on us, we need to be sure about the sovereign of our lives.

Not our emotions.

Not our desires.

Not our relationships.

Not our friends.

Not our families.

God.

If He is Lord, then we can rest easy in His care, day or night.

. . . .

Almighty Lord, You are the supreme One in my
life. Tonight, I rest in You. Amen.

HE IS GOOD

Oh, taste and see that the LORD is good;
blessed is the man who trusts in Him!
PSALM 34:8 NKJV

Did you ever wonder about something on your plate then taste it to find it was amazing?

In a way, that's the thought of Psalm 34:8. The writer admonishes us to see for ourselves how good God is. And *good* here doesn't just mean a cool experience. It means wholly excellent, through and through. There is no taint in Him.

Being convinced of God's complete goodness is reassuring. If He is good in every aspect, then He can do nothing out of a wrong motive. I can trust that He is working in my life (and in the lives of those I love) for His totally good purposes. I can know the truth of the statement, "I can trust God, not to do what I like, but to do what is right."

Sometimes our sleep is interrupted because we can't trust the people closest to us. We doubt their motives or their wisdom or their maturity. But there is no need to worry about God. We can go to bed resting in Him, since all He is and does is eternally good. And that's a good thought to sleep on!

. . . .

Lord God, You are ultimately and thoroughly good.
I trust myself and my family to You tonight. Amen.

HE IS HOLY

Yet you are holy, enthroned on the praises of Israel.
PSALM 22:3 ESV

The word *holy* denotes absolute purity. That is a picture of the God of heaven.

Good describes what He does; *holy* describes what He is. God's actions are good because His nature is holy.

For us, holiness is an acquired state—we become holy out of our relationship with God. But for Him, holiness is His eternal state of being. There has never been a time (nor will there be one) when He is not the embodiment of the term.

Tonight, you may feel the gap between yourself and God. You may recognize the fact that you are contaminated by sin and need His purity for yourself. The answer to this impassable gulf is Jesus. Because He died, in a substitute death for us, we can have His life. And all you have to do is ask.

They say there is no pillow like a clear conscience. Why don't you test the theory tonight? Confess your need to God, and let Him give you His holiness.

. . . .

God, I can't come close to You in my own goodness. Purify me tonight, and make me holy through Jesus. In His name I pray, amen.

HE IS FAITHFUL

Great is thy faithfulness.
LAMENTATIONS 3:23 KJV

If you grew up in a church where hymns were sung, even occasionally, you know the song built on this verse. It's a magnificent tribute to our God, the ever-faithful One:

Great is thy faithfulness,
O God my Father.
There is no shadow of
turning with Thee.

Faithfulness is an attribute that shines more clearly when things are going wrong. It is when we go through trials and testings that we see God's faithfulness in action. When we're in our deepest need, we see Him supply. When we are most alone, we feel His presence. When we have no other options, we watch Him make a way. When we reach the end of our resources, we experience the reality that He is enough.

It is nighttime, and you are tired—weary from the day's demands and ready for rest. In your heart, you carry needs and longings and yearnings that require capable, dependable hands. Entrust your deepest needs to God, and watch His faithfulness come through again and again.

· ·

Father in heaven, I rejoice in Your great faithfulness.
Tonight, I throw myself and my cares onto You. Amen.

HE IS NEVER LATE

He has made everything beautiful in its time.
ECCLESIASTES 3:11 AMPC

A great man once said, "God's clock keeps perfect time."

That certainly sounds good, but it's hard to believe sometimes. Remember the story of Lazarus, Mary, and Martha?

The two sisters sent word to Jesus that His good friend, their brother Lazarus, was sick. Instead of going right to him, Jesus delayed for two days. By the time He finally reached that home He loved to visit, Lazarus was dead.

Mary and Martha both correctly stated, "Lord, if You had been here, my brother would not have died." True, but this should have given the sisters a clue: since Jesus wasn't there, Lazarus *was* supposed to die at that time. Not because Jesus didn't care, but because He had a grander plan in mind.

Perhaps there are some hopes or dreams in our lives that need to die. Perhaps you are thinking of one right now as you try to go to sleep. Rest in God's timetable. Things will be beautiful when *He* is ready.

. . . .

God in heaven, Your clock never needs repairs, and it is
always in perfect synchronization with Your purpose.
Tonight, I surrender my life schedule to Yours. Amen.

HE IS ETERNAL

Before the mountains were brought forth, or ever You had formed the
earth and the world, even from everlasting to everlasting, You are God.
PSALM 90:2 NKJV

Few things in our world last a long time. In fact, it seems that we get more disposable every day.

Paper plates, contact lenses, diapers, K-cups. . .the list goes on and on.

I think this disposable mind-set affects us in our spiritual state as well. We forget that there is nothing disposable in God's kingdom. He existed as God from eternity past and will continue to exist as God forever. While He has given us eternal life, He has always possessed it. Whether or not we can fathom that, it's true.

Because God is eternal, He outlives any power or problem that we could have. And that means that there is nothing gnawing at you tonight that God can't handle. If you give your problem over to Him, He can find a way to redeem your circumstance.

Don't despair. The God who is from everlasting to everlasting invites you to give Him your troubles. Then you can fall asleep in confidence.

. . . .

God, You are eternal—and that gives me hope.
Tonight, I give You my temporal broken things.
Redeem them for Your glory. In Jesus' name, amen.

HE IS INTENTIONAL

And we know that all things work together for good to them that
love God, to them who are the called according to his purpose.
ROMANS 8:28 KJV

Many of us have heard this verse since we were little. But you **may never have thought of** it in relation to God's intentionality.

Yes, these words are a comfort to Christians facing suffering and testing. They can find reassurance in the fact that nothing is happening to them that is not, in some way, part of God's bigger plan. But it says more than that.

This verse tells us that God is intentional, that He is not haphazard in the way He runs the universe—and our lives. He does things for a reason.

The word *random* is used a lot these days. And I think the philosophy behind it has even crept into our theology. But there is nothing random about the Lord Jehovah. He is constantly at work, with a purpose in mind, pulling all the separate threads of our world into a weaving of future beauty.

What happened to you today that felt random? An incident at work? A sticky episode in a relationship? A personal trial? Lean back into God's grace tonight and remember that He is intentional. That won't take away all the difficulty, but it will help you find peace as you go to sleep.

· ·

Heavenly Father, You are a God of intention and
purpose. I find rest in that tonight. Amen.

HE NEVER SLEEPS

He Who keeps you will not slumber. Behold, He who
keeps Israel will neither slumber nor sleep.
PSALM 121:3–4 AMPC

You know that, right? You know God doesn't sleep.

He doesn't need to. He is never required to take a break, get some rest, or restore His energy. Now, we know that He did "rest" on the seventh day of Creation (see Genesis 2:2). But He did so to give us a pattern. The wording of the scripture regarding the Sabbath indicates that God's rest was a cessation from work, not a need for sleep. That's an important facet of our conversation today.

Our world and its workers continue around the clock. But nobody—not even the night owls working the graveyard shift or creating their art in the wee hours—has the stamina to go nonstop. Eventually, all of us have to take a break and sleep. We're human, not robots, and we require slumber.

But God never has a need for that. He is God! This evening, find comfort in the fact of His continual awareness of You. God never needs to rest His eyes. Whatever time of night you read this, He's completely focused—totally aware and fully engaged. You don't have to be. So get some sleep now.

. . . .

Lord, tonight I find comfort in the fact that You don't
sleep. So now I'm going to. Good night.

HE IS EVERYWHERE

*Where shall I go from your Spirit? Or where shall I flee from
your presence? If I ascend to heaven, you are there! If I make my
bed in Sheol, you are there! If I take the wings of the morning,
and dwell in the uttermost parts of the sea, even there your
hand shall lead me, and your right hand shall hold me.*

PSALM 139:7–10 ESV

We used to call it the "boonies." We meant spots in seemingly forsaken places.

In the little bit of traveling I've done, I have sometimes found myself in desolate locales. How about you? Deserted little points in the backwoods or lonely stretches of mountain road that seem like, as some say, the back side of nowhere. I've heard people use the term "godforsaken" to describe a particular place that seemed bereft of human life. . .or divine oversight.

But this is simply untrue. There is not a place on earth uninhabited by God! There is no place on this earth created by Him that He does not oversee. There is no spot where a human can hide from His awareness. Jonah surely found this out—he tried to run from the Lord's presence and found himself squarely in His sights.

Tonight, wherever you make your bed, don't let the enemy convince you that God isn't there. Nothing could be further from the truth.

. . . .

*Lord God, You are present everywhere and with
me right now. Thank You, and amen.*

HE CARES

Therefore humble yourselves under the mighty hand of God, that He may exalt you in due time, casting all your care upon Him, for He cares for you.
1 PETER 5:6–7 NKJV

We humans are pretty good at doing things halfway. And God knows it. So He inspired the apostle Peter to remind us to fully cast our troubles onto the Lord, letting Him carry them for us.

It's like my son throwing down his backpack after he comes home from school: he "casts" it down. That's how we're supposed to give our burdens to the Lord.

When any of my children come home from school, they want relief from the stress of the day. They throw down their packs, grab a snack, and often head outdoors for a time of relaxation before they begin their homework and music practice. For a few hours, they don't care what happens to the backpack—they've laid it down.

What do you have on your back, figuratively speaking, that you need to cast on the Lord? As you've gone through this day, you've gathered up troubles and stress and anxieties. God is now saying that school is over—it's time to lay down the backpack and rest in Him while you sleep.

. . . .

God my Father, You care. And because of that, I fling my backpack of cares down before You. Amen.

HE IS POWERFUL

"Behold, I am the LORD, the God of all flesh.
Is there anything too hard for Me?"
JEREMIAH 32:27 NKJV

Do you remember studying "rhetorical questions"? Those are expressions of speech in which the speaker asks something for which he or she expects no verbal response. It's more like a question to encourage thinking.

I can't say if God expected a verbal answer to this question or not. Either way, we know that answer is an emphatic "no." *Nothing* is too difficult for Him.

God has a proven track record. He can handle any kind of dilemma, any type of puzzle. Think for a moment of the issues Jesus encountered during His earthly life—uncurable diseases, violent weather, social prejudices, demonic activity, even death itself. None of these were beyond His scope of redemptive grace. Nor is anything in your life.

I don't know what you faced today. You may have been betrayed, berated, abandoned, or abused. But, hard as those things are, none of it is too difficult for Him. God can find a way for you when there seems to be none. Bring your shattered pieces to Him, because He has the power to do something good.

· ·

Father God, things are falling apart in my world, but I know You are all-
powerful. I give my jagged pieces to You tonight. In Jesus' name, amen.

HE PROTECTS

*"The LORD is my rock and my fortress and my deliverer, my God,
my rock, in whom I take refuge, my shield, and the horn of my salvation,
my stronghold and my refuge, my savior; you save me from violence."*

2 SAMUEL 22:2–3 ESV

For a while, bumper stickers and T-shirts proclaimed, "No fear." I don't think that was really true.

Some people want others to think they aren't afraid of anything. Most likely, those people are bluffing. Every human being is afraid of something; fear is a result of the fallenness of our world. Some fear creepy, crawly things like spiders and lizards; others fear scurrying things like mice; still others fear snakes or lightning or even clowns. Then there are the bigger fears, of things like disaster or death.

All of us crave protection from our fears. None of us is strong enough to provide it.

But God is the ultimate Protector! Today's verses, spoken long ago by David, use many words that indicate protection: fortress, deliverer, rock, refuge, shield, stronghold, Savior. When we trust in David's God, our biggest fears are subject to His peace working within us. Tonight, make these words your own—and don't let fear rob you of your sleep.

. . . .

*Heavenly Father, thank You for protecting me
both in body and in mind. Amen.*

HE KEEPS

*Keep me as the apple of Your eye; hide me
under the shadow of Your wings.*
PSALM 17:8 NKJV

"Mommy, keep this for me!" When my children were small, they would say that after running up with some sort of treasure gripped in a chubby hand. It might have been a shell or a rock, an acorn or a leaf. But whatever it was, it was precious to them—and they wanted to put it in the hand of one they were sure could keep it safe for them.

Today's verse talks about being kept as the apple of God's eye. Bible scholars tell us this means the pupil. One commentator has described all the ways God put protection around this important member of the body—including the skull, the eyelids, and the lashes—all in an attempt to keep harmful things out of the eye.

David, the writer of this verse, asked God to keep him in the same way. We can assume David was in some type of danger as he journeyed toward the throne of Israel, so he asked the Lord for protection.

God can keep not only our bodies but also our hearts and minds. When we rest our inner being on Him, He puts up a front of protection—and we are safe from the enemy.

* * *

*Father in heaven, tonight I need You to keep me,
both physically and spiritually. Amen.*

HE SEES

For a man's ways are before the eyes of the
LORD, and he ponders all his paths.
PROVERBS 5:21 ESV

Mothers sometimes tell their children, "I have eyes in the back of my head." And little ones might believe that. After all, they think almost anything is possible. Older children though come to realize that the phrase really means moms have a "sixth sense" about what's going on. It's almost like having special vision.

Many disasters—from household catastrophes to bad choices on the part of adolescents—have been averted because mothers sensed a problem and intervened. God has given mothers a special intuition, and much of the time it is uncannily on target.

God Himself though possesses full-surround vision, a complete scope of 360 degrees. He sees *everything*. And because of that, you and I can pillow our heads tonight in complete confidence that nothing in our lives is hidden from Him. Of course, this means that He is aware of our sins too—we must confess our failures to Him and get back on track.

As you end your nightly routine and head off to bed tonight, take a moment to be thankful for the all-seeing eyes of God. Because nothing is hidden from Him, nothing will surprise Him.

. . . .

Oh God, I praise You because You see everywhere at once.
Tonight, let me fall asleep under Your gaze. Amen.

HE REDEEMS

Bless the LORD, O my soul, and all that is within me,
bless his holy name! ... Who redeems your life from the
pit, who crowns you with steadfast love and mercy.
PSALM 103:1, 4 ESV

To *redeem* is to buy back, to restore. That's the work in which our God specializes.

I have a friend who restores vintage cars. He finds delight in bringing them back to their original, pristine condition through body work, paint, and custom detail. You might say he "redeems" these vehicles. They come to him broken and smashed, dirty and worn out. But my friend gives them new life. When they're done, people know that a master has been at work.

The Bible is full of examples of God's redemptive work. Beginning with Adam and Eve in the garden, God shows us that He doesn't throw messed-up humans away—He restores them, repairs them, and renews them. And as we go about life, everyone who knows our story has to realize that the Master has been at work.

God's redeeming work always brings honor to Him. One day, He will complete the redemption by giving us brand-new, eternal bodies. You can be sure that we'll be even better than we were in our original condition.

Go to sleep tonight knowing that God is redeeming you. And He always completes what He starts.

. . . .

Lord, I'm Yours to repair and restore. Thank You for redeeming me. Amen.

HE HOLDS

Bless our God, O peoples; let the sound of his praise be heard,
who has kept our soul among the living and has not let our feet slip.

I love to see a little girl walking beside her daddy, her little hand in his. It's a picture of trust and protection, of keeping power.

When my children were little, they would sometimes go out to the yard where my husband was working and "help" him. Of course, they didn't really do anything that made his work easier, but they were there in his presence, under his protection. If he took them anywhere on an errand, he would be sure to hold their tiny hands while they crossed the parking lots. He made sure they didn't trip over something or walk in front of a car. He was holding on to them.

Our God holds on to us too. While we can't see His big hands, we know by faith that they are there, protecting our physical lives but, more importantly, protecting our souls. Satan would use many things to make us trip, but our Father sees the danger before we do and guides us around the enemy's traps.

While you sleep tonight, your soul and your body are safe in God's keeping. Don't worry about a thing.

. . . .

Father in heaven, thank You for keeping me safe, in soul and body. Amen.

Section 4:
TUCKED IN

YOU'RE ONE OF THE CHILDREN

As a father shows compassion to his children, so the
LORD shows compassion to those who fear him.
PSALM 103:13 ESV

I'm one of those sentimental moms, I guess. I've always "tucked in" my children at night.

Now, that doesn't mean I literally wrap the covers around them and adjust their pillows—although at times I have done those things. It means I like to say a brief prayer with them as they're lying in bed, making sure they are okay to go to sleep.

I think God, our Father in heaven, likes to do that too. I believe He finds pleasure in seeing us ready for a night of rest. From His vantage point high above, He looks down on us with compassion—just like an earthly parent observes his or her own child.

Some readers may have one child in their house tonight. Others may have several. Some readers' kids may be fully grown and living on their own. And some readers may never have had children or been married. Whatever your circumstances, you are precious to your Father in heaven. As a human father shows compassion to his children, so the Lord shows compassion to those who fear Him.

. . . .

My Father, tonight I need to feel Your great arms around
me, tucking me in for a night of rest. Thank You for
making a way for me to belong to You. Amen.

COVERED OVER

But let all those who take refuge and put their trust in
You rejoice; let them ever sing and shout for joy, because
You make a covering over them and defend them.
PSALM 5:11 AMPC

When I was a child, fearful of the dark, covers were always a **great form of** protection.

You remember doing that, right?

You pulled the covers up until only your eyes showed. Then you **lay rigid in bed,** not moving a muscle—so the monsters couldn't see you. You **even tried to** breathe quietly. You watched intently. And it worked every **time. . .** at least for me. Not once was I attacked by a creature from the **shadows.**

There is something about being covered that makes us feel **protected** (**even** though my childhood idea that blankets were impenetrable **was way off base**). Those layers of soft, warm quilts on the bed provide **not only physical** but psychological comfort.

Scripture tells us that the Lord our God is a covering over **us too. He is the warmth and** protection **we need** from the fears of the **night. Reach out** to Him right now and you won't even need to try to fool those monsters in the corners!

. . . .

Lord, tonight let me take refuge in You. Put Your covering over me. Amen.

MEDITATIONS

My mouth will praise you with joyful lips, when I remember you
upon my bed, and meditate on you in the watches of the night.
PSALM 63:5–6 ESV

The hours we're lying in bed are a natural time to think. Sometimes our thoughts are positive; sometimes they're not. Before falling asleep, the mind is either winding down or gearing up—and it's natural to have significant thoughts at that time.

As a woman, I've found that those thoughts usually reflect the important facets of my life and many times spur me toward conversation. Unfortunately, men generally do not have the same verbal inclinations at bedtime. . .so what I'd like to be a conversation just doesn't happen.

Maybe it's because I never got to talk, or perhaps it's the result of a dream or indigestion or just the typical stress in the family schedule—but sometimes I wake up in the middle of the night. Whatever the reason, there are times I'm just wide awake when I should be sleeping.

The psalmist said he used those moments to meditate on the greatness of God, and I'm sure he would encourage us to follow that example. Not only can that fill our minds with Christ-centered thinking, but it may also fill the next few hours of sleep with more pleasant dreams!

. . . .

Lord, tonight I choose to meditate on You as I lie on
my bed. Rock me to sleep in Your love. Amen.

TWINKLE, TWINKLE, LITTLE STAR

He counts the number of the stars; He calls them all by name.
PSALM 147:4 NKJV

It was the first real song my daughters learned to play on the violin:

Twinkle, twinkle, little star.
How I wonder what you are!
Up above the world so high,
Like a diamond in the sky. . . .

We teach the melody to the very young, since it seems to fit their innocence and sense of curiosity about our world. As they learn more about the universe, we need to point them to the One who made it in the first place.

But even adults who know about stars and the intricacies of the heavens sometimes stand in awe at the display of beauty and intelligence in the night sky. When we gaze at the labyrinth of planets and comets and stars, we are reminded of how great God is. And this very God watches over us while we sleep through the night.

This evening, as you pass by the window on your way to bed, take a moment to look up at the sky. You may not know the names of the stars, but God does. And He knows *your* name. You can have a personal relationship with the Maker of the stars! That's the most comforting thing I know as I drift off to sleep.

Lord of the universe, thank You for making the stars.
I'd love to hear You call out their names! Amen.

BEING ALONE

I am like a pelican of the wilderness; I am like an owl of the desert.
I lie awake, and am like a sparrow alone on the housetop.
PSALM 102:6–7 NKJV

When they were smaller, my children liked to know that someone else was around as they went to sleep.

Haven't we all had that feeling during our lives? There are times we just don't want to be alone. God, after all, made us for relationship and companionship. He even said, "It is not good that man should be alone; I will make him a helper comparable to him" (Genesis 2:18 NKJV). So, from the very beginning, it was God's plan for us to live in community.

In the verse above, the animals used to illustrate aloneness were common to the people in Bible times. They would have understood the significance of the comparison.

As evening falls, the emotions that go with aloneness become more dramatic—night always magnifies our experiences. Some people may not be physically alone tonight, but they're alone emotionally. Some feel abandoned by a person who was supposed to love unconditionally.

Whatever your situation, take courage in the unfailing truth that you are never truly alone. Though you can't see a physical body, God is with you. The only thing that could keep Him away is your rejection. Embrace His presence tonight, and rest.

. . . .

Father, I know You are with me. I thank You
that I am not truly alone. Amen.

OUT OF SIGHT

"The Lord watch between you and me,
when we are out of one another's sight."
Genesis 31:49 esv

For a mother, there is nothing quite as heartrending as leaving your child and walking away. Whether it occurs at a day care, a church nursery, a bus stop, or a classroom, handing your "baby" into the care of another and removing yourself feels like abandonment. This is true even though the mom knows the separation is a natural and needful part of the child's development.

This emotion is still present when a mom leaves her son or daughter on a college campus and drives away. Though we know that young adults are fully capable of caring for themselves—and we are assured that God their heavenly Father is right there with them—we still wipe tears from our eyes as we watch them step into life on their own.

The important thing is that God watches over our loved ones in the gap between our together times. It may not be children you're missing tonight—perhaps it's a good friend who had to move, or family members in another state or country. But whatever the particulars, God can watch between you until you're all together again.

That's a comforting thought on which to sleep tonight.

. . . .

Father God, please watch over the ones I love who are
not with me tonight. In Jesus' name, amen.

THE MAN IN THE MOON

He appointed the moon for seasons.
PSALM 104:19 NKJV

It's something we point out to little children: "See the man in the moon!" To be honest, it took me a while, as an adult, to really perceive the outlines of the eyes and nose and mouth in those lunar craters.

The moon has captivated mankind since the beginning. Perhaps it's because we can gaze at this glowing orb in the sky in a way that we cannot do with the sun. Down through the millennia, staring at the moon has generated within humans the desire to touch it, to explore it, to walk on it. In the late 1960s, after much trial and error and disaster and danger, this was accomplished—God actually allowed His human creation to travel to another celestial body. That always awes me.

The Bible tells us that God made the moon for specific reasons—not only for beauty and awe but also for practical things like controlling the tides and directing the seasons. Or, as the Bible says, "to rule the night" (Genesis 1:16 NKJV).

I don't know what is going on in your house tonight. But outside, there is a glowing reminder that God thinks of everything. You can trust Him tonight as you sleep.

. . . .

*Lord God, I love Your moon. Thank You for Your
creation and Your presence. Amen.*

THE CONFIDENCE TO REST

In the fear of the LORD one has strong confidence,
and his children will have a refuge.
PROVERBS 14:26 ESV

Do you know what all the ads and commercials for **home-security systems have in** common?

They strike at a visceral need for all of us—the desire to be **confident in our** safety.

Nobody wants to be violated by intruders during the night. **The companies** that sell these systems realize that and craft their selling **strategies around** it. And we *should* be careful—our world is inhabited by some **whose hearts** are driven by greed or desperation, people who will take **whatever they can,** from whomever they can.

Yet the writer of Proverbs tells us that for our minds and hearts, **there is confidence** in the "fear of the Lord." That's not the same kind **of fear that** home-security systems address; it's a reverence for our **worthy and honorable** God. When we **keep** Him in His rightful place, we **are secure. And He is a** place of refuge.

I hope you live in a **safe place,** whether that's on a **quiet street or a** country road, or perhaps in a studio apartment or high-rise in the city. But wherever you find yourself tonight, God is your confidence and refuge.

· ·

Father God, watch over me while I sleep. I reverence
You tonight and trust in You. Amen.

LEAVE A LIGHT ON

"For You are my lamp, O LORD; the LORD shall enlighten my darkness."
2 SAMUEL 22:29 NKJV

For years, a popular motel chain had as its slogan, "We'll leave the light on for you." It was catchy, and it spoke to the psyche.

Something about "leaving a light on" speaks of welcome and love. It may be a lighted front porch, a lamp in a window, or a candle burning on a mantel—the image of a light left on is powerful.

Children especially are fond of lights at night, a fact that speaks to their common fear of the dark. A nightlight in the hall or a corner of the room reassures kids that the darkness is not complete—there is still light somewhere. I confess that even as an adult I don't like a pitch-black house at night. And if you've ever gotten up in the darkness and couldn't find your way to the bathroom or rammed your foot into an unexpected item on the floor, you probably like a little light somewhere too.

The Bible tells us that God *is* light. Because of that, He can bring illumination—in a spiritual sense—to any situation we face. Today's verse reminds us that He is the lamp we need for light. . .welcoming, warming, and guiding. That's the best kind of nightlight to have!

. . . .

Father in heaven, keep Your light burning in
my life tonight and tomorrow. Amen.

Section 5:
GIFTS OF SLEEP

WIDE-AWAKE EYES

*Consider and answer me, O Lord my God; light up
my eyes, lest I sleep the sleep of death.*
PSALM 13:3 ESV

It's hard to give an exact attribution for the saying, "The eyes are the window to the soul." But whoever first strung those words together probably got the idea from scripture. Ecclesiastes 12:3 (ESV), using metaphors for aging, says of the eyes that "those who look through the windows are dimmed."

Eyes tell a lot about us. They give clues to our emotions. They denote intelligence and humor—you really can see a twinkle in the eye! They reveal trauma (the eyes of Holocaust survivors and prisoners of war often have a haunted look). They can brighten with happiness or darken with anger. They can look softly at someone who is loved or grow cold in the presence of an enemy. The eyes can even show consciousness. Yes, God made the eyes to do much more than serve as cameras for our brains. Our eyes are our souls on display.

Since our eyes reveal so much about us, they will tattle on us if we're cheating ourselves of sleep. Bags and sags and shadows will tell everyone that we're not resting properly! Let's be good stewards tonight of the bodies God gave us, and tomorrow our eyes will thank us for it.

- -

*Thank You, Father, for the eyes You gave me. Now I'm going to
rest them so they can shine brightly for You tomorrow! Amen.*

REWARDED BY ENERGY

"God is my strength and power, and He makes my way perfect."
2 SAMUEL 22:33 NKJV

When I was a freshman in college, I remember taking over-the-counter pills called No Doz that were packed with caffeine. They were touted as an aid to keep you alert and awake. As a typical freshman, pulling a few all-nighters, I tried them out. After one episode where I felt so revved up that climbing the walls seemed like a good idea, I removed the pills from my routine. But today there are many other options for those who need a quick boost of energy.

To be honest, I've never drunk any of those little bottles with all their great promises. I don't know if they work or not. And I'm sure there are certain circumstances where they might come in handy for one reason or another. But I do know there is no substitute for a good night's sleep. God designed our bodies to work best when we're renewing our bodily energy His way.

God is the source of all energy, of course, and the only One who can give us spiritual strength. So we look to Him to energize our souls, to give us daily power over temptation, and to provide the grace to conquer our challenges. Let's acknowledge how He made us, and do our best to get our eight hours every night. That's a recipe for energy on all counts.

. . . .

God, I thank You for the strength to live.
Restore me tonight while I sleep. Amen.

FOCUSED THOUGHTS

How great are your works, O LORD! Your thoughts are very deep!

For Navy SEALs, the most torturous part of training is "Hell Week." During this grinding part of their preparation, they must stay awake for five-plus days, participating in rigorous activities all the while. They really know the meaning of sleep deprivation.

A debilitating effect of lack of sleep is an inability to focus. The mind becomes hazy as the brain loses sharpness due to fatigue. Most people can still function, but they are not at their optimum level of clarity and creativity. SEAL units have to keep going even with foggy minds and exhausted bodies, so their trainers push them to the limits of endurance. For most of us though, our excuses for sleep deprivation are considerably more self-centered—we want to stay up late to finish something we enjoy or we just love to socialize, for example.

Our God is a being of deep thoughts. And He made us in His image. In order to be at our best—and to function at full capacity for His glory—we need to make sure we are not routinely short-circuiting the rest cycles we need. Let's surrender to His keeping at night, so we can think His thoughts in the morning.

. . . .

*Lord, I rest myself in You tonight, so I can focus my
thoughts for Your glory tomorrow. Amen.*

CALMNESS

Meditate within your heart on your bed, and be still.
PSALM 4:4 NKJV

One of the gifts of sleep is a calmed outlook.

Sleep is the antidote to tension. And we have an overload of tension in our world right now. Just listening to the news on the morning commute is enough to give us loads of unrest.

What's going to happen in politics?

What if the Dow Jones tumbles?

What if rogue nations gain nuclear power?

What if these school shootings don't stop?

What if the weather cycle gets any crazier?

The psalmist says to meditate within your heart while you lie in bed. And *be still.*

That is one of the most difficult disciplines for us in the twenty-first century. Yet God tells us in Psalm 46:10 (NKJV) to "be still, and know" that He is God. There is something to this thing of learning quietness.

Perhaps, with practice, we can make our bedtime a quiet time in which to reflect and meditate. That would sure beat the ruckus that often accompanies the end of a harried day.

Tonight, turn off your news reports, your music, and your social media, and spend a few moments in quiet meditation. Be still.

. . . .

Lord God, I quiet my heart before You tonight. Help me to release the tension of this day and find calm in You. Amen.

BETTER THAN THE SPA

I lay down and slept; I woke again, for the LORD sustained me.
PSALM 3:5 ESV

I've always wanted to visit a spa. You know, one of those spas by the ocean—with stone floors, lush Egyptian cotton towels, vibrant greenery in every corner, and white-coated attendants close by. And then those heated rocks they put down your back after a massage. Ah, it sounds like the ultimate luxury. I think I would sleep beautifully then.

But today's verse was written during one of the most turbulent times in David's reign. He was running from his own son, Absalom, who was trying to take over the kingdom. David was the prey in his own realm. And yet, in the midst of this, he said that he laid down and slept and awoke refreshed, because God had sustained him during the night.

You can't find a spa treatment better than that. To refresh and nourish is the goal of a spa—but God accomplished it for David without the towels and rocks.

I don't know what trouble you're running from tonight. But I know that the God of heaven who supported David can support you while you sleep.

. . . .

Heavenly Father, I'm just at home, not at the spa—
but I ask You to refresh me tonight while I sleep. Amen.

Section 6:
SLEEPERS IN THE BIBLE

SISERA: APPOINTED TIME

However, Sisera had fled away on foot to the tent of Jael. . . . And Jael went out to meet Sisera, and said to him, "Turn aside, my lord, turn aside to me; do not fear." And when he had turned aside with her into the tent, she covered him with a blanket. Then he said to her, "Please give me a little water to drink, for I am thirsty." So she opened a jug of milk, gave him a drink, and covered him. Then Jael, Heber's wife, took a tent peg and took a hammer in her hand, and went softly to him and drove the peg into his temple, and it went down into the ground; for he was fast asleep and weary. So he died.
JUDGES 4:17–19, 21 NKJV

I admit that this is a strange passage to include in a book of devotions for peaceful sleep. That certainly wasn't Sisera's experience, and his story is, quite frankly, gruesome.

But this story also shows God working for His people, and that fact does enhance our rest. Sisera was the commander of the army of King Jabin, who was oppressing the Israelites. God provided a deliverer for the people in the person of Deborah, who led the battle against Sisera's forces. And God used a simple housewife, Jael, to seal the Israelites' victory.

Don't worry tonight about the "bad guys." God can handle them.

. . . .

Lord, please help me to trust You with my fears.
I know You can handle them all. Amen.

EUTYCHUS: LOYAL LISTENER

And there sat in a window a certain young man named Eutychus,
being fallen into a deep sleep: and as Paul was long preaching,
he sunk down with sleep, and fell down from the third loft, and was
taken up dead. And Paul went down, and fell on him, and embracing
him said, Trouble not yourselves; for his life is in him. When he
therefore was come up again, and had broken bread, and eaten,
and talked a long while, even till break of day, so he departed. And
they brought the young man alive, and were not a little comforted.
ACTS 20:9–12 KJV

Long-winded preachers are the theme of good-natured teasing in church circles. But beyond this young man mentioned in Acts, I've never heard of anyone else almost dying as a result of a long sermon. The fact that he is named is significant—it makes you wonder if he gained a sort of notoriety from this experience: "The Man Almost Killed by a Sermon," or something like that.

I'm sure his fall from the loft caused a commotion in the service. Paul stopped preaching long enough to restore the young man's life and take a meal then got back to his sermon.

It's not a bad thing to slip out of consciousness while listening to God's Word. You can get an app for your phone or device that allows you to do that. And the nice thing is that as you lay in bed listening, you won't have to worry about falling—except to sleep.

. . . .

Lord, make my devotion to Your Word to be like that which Eutychus
showed—willing to learn about You until sleep overtakes me. Amen.

URIAH: SACRIFICIAL SLEEP

So David sent word to Joab, "Send me Uriah the Hittite." And Joab sent Uriah to David. When Uriah came to him, David asked how Joab was doing and how the people were doing and how the war was going. Then David said to Uriah, "Go down to your house and wash your feet." And Uriah went out of the king's house, and there followed him a present from the king. But Uriah slept at the door of the king's house with all the servants of his lord, and did not go down to his house.

2 SAMUEL 11:6–9 ESV

A man on active military duty, especially one on the front lines, is probably sleep-deprived. And sleep deprivation can make human beings do strange things. It can relax the usual inhibitions a person feels, causing him to be less cautious in his decisions.

The chance to sleep at home would be a luxury for any enlisted man. But David's valiant soldier Uriah lived by a code of honor. He refused to indulge in the comforts of home when his buddies on the battlefield could not. Sadly, due to David's selfish sin, that honor cost Uriah his life.

As you lay down to sleep tonight, such stakes are probably not involved in your life. But let's commit—even in a state of exhaustion—to cling to our honor like Uriah did, doing what is right even when it costs.

. . . .

Lord, give me the moral fiber to make honorable decisions, even when I'm tired. Amen.

SAUL: GOD'S ANOINTED

So David and Abishai went to the army by night. And there lay Saul sleeping within the encampment, with his spear stuck in the ground at his head, and Abner and the army lay around him. Then Abishai said to David, "God has given your enemy into your hand this day. Now please let me pin him to the earth with one stroke of the spear, and I will not strike him twice." But David said to Abishai, "Do not destroy him, for who can put out his hand against the LORD's anointed and be guiltless?" And David said, "As the LORD lives, the LORD will strike him, or his day will come to die, or he will go down into battle and perish. The LORD forbid that I should put out my hand against the LORD's anointed."

1 SAMUEL 26:7–11 ESV

It is not uncommon for a murder to occur while the victim is sleeping. Though some killers want their victims to know what is happening, others are happy to strike when the target is unaware of his or her fate.

Abishai, David's commander, saw an opportunity to end King Saul's reign of terror over the man destined to be Israel's next king. It seemed to be God-given—Saul was asleep, the two men had a spear, and they were standing right over the king. But David disagreed. He knew that God's precepts stand fast no matter how "right" our human arguments may seem. He would not raise his hand against the anointed king. David allowed Saul to sleep through the night, trusting God to exchange leaders in His right time.

· ·

Father God, vengeance is Yours. May I honor Your Word no matter the opportunity. Amen.

THE BRIDESMAIDS: UNPREPARED SLEEPERS

"Then the kingdom of heaven will be like ten virgins who took their lamps and went to meet the bridegroom. Five of them were foolish, and five were wise. For when the foolish took their lamps, they took no oil with them, but the wise took flasks of oil with their lamps. As the bridegroom was delayed, they all became drowsy and slept. But at midnight there was a cry, 'Here is the bridegroom! Come out to meet him'. . . . Watch therefore, for you know neither the day nor the hour."

MATTHEW 25:1–6, 13 ESV

There is a time and place for sleep. Waiting for a bridal party is generally not that time or place.

The girls in this parable of Jesus' were honoring a tradition observed in ancient Jewish weddings: friends of the couple would wait for the procession to arrive then join in the celebration. Middle Eastern countries are more lenient in their observance of time, and evidently this bridegroom was taking longer to collect his bride than anyone had anticipated. The maids got drowsy and fell off to sleep.

There is, of course, a spiritual application to this story. As we wait on the coming of our Lord, we must be prepared, having our "lamps" ready and not forgetting the "oil" of the Holy Spirit to keep our faith vibrant. As you prepare for your physical rest, pray that God will always keep you spiritually alert.

. . . .

Lord Jesus, You are the Bridegroom and You are coming for Your Church. I want to be part of that celebration. Amen.

THE DISCIPLES: LOW RESOLVE

Then He said to them, "My soul is exceedingly sorrowful,
even to death. Stay here and watch with Me." He went a
little farther and fell on His face, and prayed, saying, "O My
Father, if it is possible, let this cup pass from Me; nevertheless,
not as I will, but as You will." Then He came to the disciples and
found them sleeping, and said to Peter, "What! Could you not
watch with Me one hour? Watch and pray, lest you enter into
temptation. The spirit indeed is willing, but the flesh is weak."
MATTHEW 26:38–41 NKJV

Jesus took His three closest friends deeper into the Garden, asking them to pray with Him. Isn't it interesting that even the Son of God wanted prayer partnership while He was here on earth?

Peter, James, and John were Jesus' closest allies, His beloved followers, His friends. He went a little farther away and began to pray, in great agony of spirit. The disciples prayed for a while. But they became sleepy and—not understanding the significance of the night—drifted off to sleep.

When Jesus returned and found His friends napping, He certainly understood their human tiredness. But He was asking them to persevere, to stand in the gap with Him as Satan advanced.

Tonight, you might need to ponder what Jesus is asking of you. Do you have the inner resolve to follow Him, even into the Garden?

. . . .

God, let my determination to follow You be strong enough
to obey whatever You ask me to do. Amen.

RUTH: TAKING RISKS

At midnight the man was startled and turned over, and behold, a woman lay at his feet! He said, "Who are you?" And she answered, "I am Ruth, your servant. Spread your wings over your servant, for you are a redeemer." And he said, "May you be blessed by the Lord, my daughter. You have made this last kindness greater than the first in that you have not gone after young men, whether poor or rich. And now, my daughter, do not fear. I will do for you all that you ask, for all my fellow townsmen know that you are a worthy woman. And now it is true that I am a redeemer. Yet there is a redeemer nearer than I. Remain tonight, and in the morning, if he will redeem you, good; let him do it. But if he is not willing to redeem you, then, as the Lord lives, I will redeem you. Lie down until the morning."

RUTH 3:8–13 ESV

The romance of Ruth and Boaz is one of those fun stories in the Bible. Boaz was a Jew; Ruth was a foreigner, a pagan. Boaz was rich and she was poor. He was the employer and she was the employee. He was older and she was young. But God's plan won out (which shouldn't surprise us) and they got together in the end.

From this nighttime encounter came a marriage and a family line that produced kings—including the King of kings, Jesus Christ.

. . . .

Heavenly Father, sometimes You ask me to do something that seems risky and uncomfortable. Help me to obey. In Jesus' name, amen.

JONAH: SLEEP OF REBELLION

Now the word of the LORD came to Jonah the son of Amittai, saying, "Arise, go to Nineveh, that great city, and cry out against it; for their wickedness has come up before Me." But Jonah arose to flee to Tarshish from the presence of the LORD. He went down to Joppa, and found a ship going to Tarshish; so he paid the fare, and went down into it, to go with them to Tarshish from the presence of the LORD. But the LORD sent out a great wind on the sea, and there was a mighty tempest on the sea, so that the ship was about to be broken up. . . . But Jonah had gone down into the lowest parts of the ship, had lain down and was fast asleep. So the captain came to him, and said to him, "What do you mean, sleeper? Arise, call on your God; perhaps your God will consider us, so that we may not perish." And they said to one another, "Come, let us cast lots, that we may know for whose cause this trouble has come upon us." So they cast lots, and the lot fell on Jonah.

JONAH 1:1–7 NKJV

It's one of the first Bible stories to capture the attention of little kids—the man swallowed whole by a fish. But the story of Jonah teaches a lot more. One simple lesson for our purposes: our rest will be disturbed if we are running from God.

. . . .

Father God, I surrender my will to You.
Help me say yes to my Nineveh. Amen.

AHASUERUS: FITFUL SLEEPER

That night the king could not sleep. So one was commanded to bring
the book of the records of the chronicles; and they were read before
the king. And it was found written that Mordecai had told of Bigthana
and Teresh, two of the king's eunuchs, the doorkeepers who had sought
to lay hands on King Ahasuerus. Then the king said, "What honor
or dignity has been bestowed on Mordecai for this?" And the king's
servants who attended him said, "Nothing has been done for him."
ESTHER 6:1–3 NKJV

As we view stories in the Bible from our long-range perspective, we can see how God works in seeming coincidence. He has a plan for our nights, and sometimes that means our *not* sleeping.

For Ahasuerus, what might have been insomnia or indigestion was actually God keeping the king awake. Why? So he would call for the royal records and discover this incident involving Mordecai. To save His people from extinction, God planned even tiny details like keeping a king from sleeping. And today we can see how everything in the story of Esther fits together.

God works similarly in our lives. The often mundane details of our lives can seem random, but we just can't see the pattern that God is weaving. Most of us would never think that God could work through our night of fitful sleep—but there is nothing too simple or humble for His plan.

Father God, help me to remember that You are often found
in the mundane as well as the profound. Amen.

DANIEL: SLEPT WITH LIONS

Then, at break of day, the king arose and went in haste to the den of lions. As he came near to the den where Daniel was, he cried out in a tone of anguish. The king declared to Daniel, "O Daniel, servant of the living God, has your God, whom you serve continually, been able to deliver you from the lions?" Then Daniel said to the king, "O king, live forever! My God sent his angel and shut the lions' mouths, and they have not harmed me, because I was found blameless before him; and also before you, O king, I have done no harm."

DANIEL 6:19–22 ESV

I'm sure Daniel would never had thought his commitment to **excellence, his integrity,** and his moral character would lead to a criminal **sentence. But they** did.

Spending the night in a den of lions would have to be one of the **most frightening** things imaginable. It was probably pitch black, cold, **strewn with** human bones, and smelling of excrement. Certainly a **dank and unpleasant** place to die.

But God came through, shutting the mouths of those who **would destroy His servant.** I don't know if Daniel slept or not that night, **but he certainly** didn't have to worry about a sudden attack. God **was on the scene, and** everything was fine.

. . . .

Lord, when I find myself in circumstances that seem dire and unfixable, I ask for Your grace. Amen.

ADAM: SLEEP OF SURPRISE

*The man gave names to all livestock and to the birds of the heavens
and to every beast of the field. But for Adam there was not found
a helper fit for him. So the LORD God caused a deep sleep to fall
upon the man, and while he slept took one of his ribs and closed up
its place with flesh. And the rib that the LORD God had taken from
the man he made into a woman and brought her to the man.*

GENESIS 2:20–22 ESV

It's the first recorded episode of sleep in the Bible.

Adam couldn't find a companion, another human, a wife. So God made
one from Adam's own body. And to do that, God caused a kind of coma to
come over the man. Imagine Adam, suddenly feeling sleepy, yawning and
lying down under a tree in the garden. Then God opens him up, takes out a
rib, and closes the wound again. This is divine surgery—no tools required,
and no need for recovery.

From the man's rib, God formed a woman. Then He brought her to
Adam. Was Adam still sleeping? Possibly. If so, did God wake him up with
a nudge? Did He talk with Eve as He led her to Adam? Did He let her in on
the surprise the man was going to have?

We don't know for sure. But we can say with confidence that this was
probably the most life-changing sleep ever!

. . . .

*Creator God, thank You for the work You do while I
sleep. I'm thankful, like Adam was. Amen.*

SAMSON: FROM SLEEP TO PRISON

When Delilah saw that he had told her all his heart, she sent and called for the lords of the Philistines, saying, "Come up once more, for he has told me all his heart." So the lords of the Philistines came up to her and brought the money in their hand. Then she lulled him to sleep on her knees, and called for a man and had him shave off the seven locks of his head. Then she began to torment him, and his strength left him. And she said, "The Philistines are upon you, Samson!" So he awoke from his sleep, and said, "I will go out as before, at other times, and shake myself free!" But he did not know that the LORD had departed from him. Then the Philistines took him and put out his eyes, and brought him down to Gaza. They bound him with bronze fetters, and he became a grinder in the prison.

JUDGES 16:18–21 NKJV

You'd think Samson would know better than to fall asleep around **Delilah**. After all, she had tried this three other times, and Samson's enemies **had been** nearby to try to overpower him. Either he really didn't **think she would betray** him or, despite his vows to God, he figured he **could retain his strength** anyway. It appears that Samson was just incredibly **arrogant,** an attitude that cost him his strength, his dignity, his eyes—and ultimately his life.

Samson's case is extreme, but just a little bit of arrogance can trip us up. Tonight, as you retire, ask God if you're harboring even a mustard seed of pride. If so, confess it—and sleep in peace.

. . . .

Oh God, let me not flout Your Word but keep my vows to You. Amen.

PETER: RESCUED WHILE SLEEPING

So Peter was kept in prison, but earnest prayer for him was made to God by the church. Now when Herod was about to bring him out, on that very night, Peter was sleeping between two soldiers, bound with two chains, and sentries before the door were guarding the prison. And behold, an angel of the Lord stood next to him, and a light shone in the cell. He struck Peter on the side and woke him, saying, "Get up quickly." And the chains fell off his hands. And the angel said to him, "Dress yourself and put on your sandals." And he did so. And he said to him, "Wrap your cloak around you and follow me." And he went out and followed him. He did not know that what was being done by the angel was real, but thought he was seeing a vision.

ACTS 12:5–9 ESV

Peter was sleeping, and the church was praying.

Herod must have feared the power of the Christians. He had Peter chained between two guards and also posted sentries outside the door. It's as if the king knew something strong was at work here.

If you're in a prison cell unjustly, it has to be encouraging to be awakened by an angel! Peter was delivered from his captors that night and brought to the place where the believers were praying. All in a night's work for an angel—always under God's care are we.

. . . .

Father, You work when the saints pray, sending angels in the night. I praise Your power this evening. Amen.

TRANSFIGURATION: WAKING UP TO GLORY

Now about eight days after these sayings he took with him Peter and John and James and went up on the mountain to pray. And as he was praying, the appearance of his face was altered, and his clothing became dazzling white. And behold, two men were talking with him, Moses and Elijah, who appeared in glory and spoke of his departure, which he was about to accomplish at Jerusalem. Now Peter and those who were with him were heavy with sleep, but when they became fully awake they saw his glory and the two men who stood with him.

LUKE 9:28–32 ESV

Many times when Jesus had something important for His disciples to experience, they were sleepy.

Let's not forget that our Enemy is more than happy to play on our human weaknesses, trying to get us to miss what God is doing. In this case, Peter, James, and John almost missed seeing the brilliant glory of Christ.

What is God doing in your life right now? He is always showing His power, in one way or another. Don't be too groggy to realize what's happening. Don't miss the transforming event about to take place.

. . . .

Father God, let my sleep be at the proper times.
Please help me to not be spiritually sleepy when You
are about to work. Show me Your glory! Amen.

Section 7:
DREAMERS IN THE BIBLE
DREAMS ARE FOR LEARNING

*"For God speaks in one way, and in two, though man **does not**
perceive it. In a dream, in a vision of the night, when **deep**
sleep falls on men, while they slumber on their beds."*

JOB 33:14–15 ESV

It was a common way for God to speak in ancient times.

Often in scripture, we read of someone instructed by God in a **dream or**
vision. They were usually vivid occurrences, and the news they carried **was**
always important. People who did not know Jehovah needed an **interpreter**
who did follow the Lord. The message was convincing and always came **true.**

God doesn't have to use dreams these days. Since Pentecost, **we have**
the Holy Spirit to instruct and guide us. As Jesus said, "I will ask the **Father,**
and he will give you another Helper, to be with you forever, even the **Spirit**
of truth" (John 14:16–17 ESV). His work of continually illuminating **our**
understanding and directing us through scripture is better than **dreams**
in the night.

Does this mean God never uses dreams now?

No, but we **need** to be cautious when considering our **own** dreams. If
they're not backed up by God's Word, we should probably leave them alone.
Let's depend instead on the solid leading of the Spirit.

· ·

Heavenly Father, thank You for sending Your Spirit to Earth to indwell
believers. I open myself up to His guidance and counsel. Amen.

ABIMELECH: PAGAN KING

*Abraham said of Sarah his wife, "She is my sister." And Abimelech king of Gerar sent and took Sarah. But God came to Abimelech in a dream by night and said to him, "Behold, you are a dead man because of the woman whom you have taken, for she is a man's wife." Now Abimelech had not approached her. So he said, "Lord, will you kill **an innocent people**? Did he not himself say to me, 'She is my sister'? And she **herself** said, 'He is my brother.' In the integrity of my heart and the **innocence** of my hands I have done this." Then God said to him in the dream, "Yes, I know that you have done this in the integrity of your heart, and it was I who kept you from sinning against me. Therefore I did not **let** you touch her. Now then, return the man's wife, for he is a prophet, so that he will pray for you, and you shall live. But if you do not return her, know that you shall surely die, you and all who are yours."*

Genesis 20:2–7 esv

It **really** was Abraham's fault: he lied. Though you could **also blame Abimelech**, who was greedy for women. And you could even **fault Sarah.** Yes, she was *that* beautiful in her old age.

But God chose to set things right when the players didn't follow the rules. The Lord was fair even to a heathen king! In this little nighttime drama, we learn to trust the integrity of our God.

. . . .

Lord, You are righteous in every way. Amen.

JOSEPH: HATED BROTHER

Now Joseph had a dream, and he told it to his brothers; and they hated him even more. So he said to them, "Please hear this dream which I have dreamed: There we were, binding sheaves in the field. Then behold, my sheaf arose and also stood upright; and indeed your sheaves stood all around and bowed down to my sheaf." And his brothers said to him, "Shall you indeed reign over us? Or shall you indeed have dominion over us?" So they hated him even more for his dreams and for his words. Then he dreamed still another dream and told it to his brothers, and said, "Look, I have dreamed another dream. And this time, the sun, the moon, and the eleven stars bowed down to me." So he told it to his father and his brothers; and his father rebuked him and said to him, "What is this dream that you have dreamed? Shall your mother and I and your brothers indeed come to bow down to the earth before you?"

GENESIS 37:5–10 NKJV

Siblings rarely appreciate one another's wisdom. Joseph's brothers surely didn't. He seemed to them to be arrogant and condescending, especially when they knew that their father preferred Joseph over the rest of them. But God used the brothers' hatred—the hatred that flared over Joseph's dreams—as the very thing that started the young man's journey to leadership and the eventual salvation of his dumbstruck siblings.

That's so like our Lord.

God, hate is never from You. Give me grace with those who will irritate me tomorrow. Amen.

THE KING'S CUPBEARER AND THE BAKER: OFFENSIVE OFFICIALS

And one night they both dreamed—the cupbearer and the baker of the king of Egypt, who were confined in the prison—each his own dream, and each dream with its own interpretation. When Joseph came to them in the morning, he saw that they were troubled. So he asked Pharaoh's officers who were with him in custody in his master's house, "Why are your faces downcast today?" They said to him, "We have had dreams, and there is no one to interpret them." And Joseph said to them, "Do not interpretations belong to God? Please tell them to me."
GENESIS 40:5–8 ESV

Dreams in the Bible didn't always bring good news. These guys in prison with Joseph found that out.

God showed each one his future in a dream. The baker must have really upset the Egyptian king—he wasn't going to make it back to the royal pastry counter. He was executed. The cupbearer though must have had something going for him, because Pharaoh decided he wanted the man around. The king restored him to his position in the palace.

These men had to dream dreams so they could meet Joseph. Then God would use that meeting later for Joseph's good. Know this: however bad a situation may look to us, God sees several steps ahead, and works all things for the good of His children.

. . . .

Father, You use the experiences of others for my good too. You work in all the details. Amen.

PHARAOH: ROYAL DREAMER

Then it came to pass, at the end of two full years, that Pharaoh had a dream.... Now it came to pass in the morning that his spirit was troubled, and he sent and called for all the magicians of Egypt and all its wise men. And Pharaoh told them his dreams, but there was no one who could interpret them for Pharaoh. Then the chief butler spoke to Pharaoh, saying: "I remember my faults this day.... Now there was a young Hebrew man with us there, a servant of the captain of the guard. And we told him, and he interpreted our dreams for us; to each man he interpreted according to his own dream."... Then Pharaoh sent and called Joseph, and they brought him quickly out of the dungeon; and he shaved, changed his clothing, and came to Pharaoh. And Pharaoh said to Joseph, "I have had a dream, and there is no one who can interpret it. But I have heard it said of you that you can understand a dream, to interpret it." So Joseph answered Pharaoh, saying, "It is not in me; God will give Pharaoh an answer of peace."
GENESIS 41:1, 8–9, 12, 14–16 NKJV

Pharaohs had immense power, and equally large egos. But this one was humble enough to ask for help when bizarre dreams troubled his sleep. Enter Joseph, a dreamer himself, who interpreted the king's dreams by the wisdom of God.

If some riddle of life is interfering with your sleep tonight, maybe you need to find a Joseph. Ask God who you could approach tomorrow for advice. Then rest in God's peace.

. . . .

*Lord, work through the events of my life,
and help me not to be arrogant. Amen.*

JACOB: FRUSTRATED WANDERER

Jacob left Beersheba and went toward Haran. And he came to a certain place and stayed there that night, because the sun had set. Taking one of the stones of the place, he put it under his head and lay down in that place to sleep. And he dreamed, and behold, there was a ladder set up on the earth, and the top of it reached to heaven. And behold, the angels of God were ascending and descending on it! And behold, the LORD stood above it and said, "I am the LORD, the God of Abraham your father and the God of Isaac. The land on which you lie I will give to you and to your offspring."

GENESIS 28:10–13 ESV

Sometimes you wonder why Jacob is such an important character in the Bible.

His mother groomed him to usurp his older brother's place as head of the family. He used shady practices to trick his brother, his father, and his employer. As a newlywed, he got a taste of his own medicine from his deceitful father-in-law. As a husband, he played favorites with his two wives. Almost without exception, Jacob was selfish and dishonest.

But God doesn't throw people away. He continued to work in Jacob's life, and this dream of heavenly angels is evidence of that. God was proving who He was and giving Jacob a chance to be part of a bigger story, one that truly changed the world. Each of us has a role to play in that story too.

. . . .

Lord, You work in ways I don't understand.
Tonight, I bring my own contradictions to You. Amen.

GIDEON: EAVESDROPPER

When Gideon came, behold, a man was telling a dream to his comrade. And he said, "Behold, I dreamed a dream, and behold, a cake of barley bread tumbled into the camp of Midian and came to the tent and struck it so that it fell and turned it upside down, so that the tent lay flat." And his comrade answered, "This is no other than the sword of Gideon the son of Joash, a man of Israel; God has given into his hand Midian and all the camp." As soon as Gideon heard the telling of the dream and its interpretation, he worshiped.

JUDGES 7:13–15 ESV

If only God would let us overhear talk of our victories before they happen!

Wouldn't that make life better? Well, maybe not. If we already knew the outcome of events, we wouldn't need faith—and we wouldn't experience the thrill of seeing how God brings His plan to pass.

But in this case, God did choose to give a little courage boost. He allowed Gideon to overhear a conversation foretelling the result of an upcoming battle. We could envy Gideon, but the story might actually indicate that Gideon was weak in faith.

As you drift off to sleep tonight, forget about the outcome of your "battle." Just trust God with what He's asked you to do tomorrow!

. . . .

Lord, You are sovereign in my life. I give all my battles to You. Amen.

SOLOMON: ASKING WISELY

At Gibeon the LORD appeared to Solomon in a dream by night; and God said, "Ask! What shall I give you?" And Solomon said: "You have shown great mercy to Your servant David my father, because he walked before You in truth, in righteousness, and in uprightness of heart with You; You have continued this great kindness for him, and You have given him a son to sit on his throne, as it is this day. Now, O LORD my God, You have made Your servant king instead of my father David, but I am a little child; I do not know how to go out or come in. And Your servant is in the midst of Your people whom You have chosen, a great people, too numerous to be numbered or counted. Therefore give to Your servant an understanding heart to judge Your people, that I may discern between good and evil. For who is able to judge this great people of Yours?" The speech pleased the Lord, that Solomon had asked this thing.

1 KINGS 3:5–10 NKJV

Genies in a bottle are make-believe. But *God* giving you the choice of any wish? Wow, Solomon was a man in a rare circumstance.

He showed that he was already a man of discernment by the nature of his request—he didn't ask for wealth or fame or position, but for wisdom. And God was so pleased He threw in the other stuff for good measure!

Tonight, we can make the same request of God. If you're not sure about that, look up James 1:5.

. . . .

Lord, I probably won't be a Solomon, but please give me wisdom to live tomorrow. In Jesus' name, amen.

NEBUCHADNEZZAR: KING ON THE BRINK

In the second year of the reign of Nebuchadnezzar, Nebuchadnezzar had dreams; his spirit was troubled, and his sleep left him. . . . The king declared to Daniel, whose name was Belteshazzar, "Are you able to make known to me the dream that I have seen and its interpretation?" Daniel answered the king and said, "No wise men, enchanters, magicians, or astrologers can show to the king the mystery that the king has asked, but there is a God in heaven who reveals mysteries, and he has made known to King Nebuchadnezzar what will be in the latter days."

DANIEL 2:1, 26–28 ESV

It amazes (and amuses) me that pagan kings were so thrilled to hear the interpretation of their dreams even when the news was not good! Nebuchadnezzar fell down and paid homage to Daniel after he had explained the king's dream of a giant statue.

The dream was of a kingdom in decline. God gave Daniel the interpretation and the skill to share it with Nebuchadnezzar. . .and Daniel grew in prominence in Babylon.

Even in the Israelites' captivity, God was working in many ways. Rest assured, tonight, that He's working in your life too.

. . . .

God, let me hunger after Your will as eagerly as pagan kings desired the interpretation of their dreams. Amen.

DANIEL: TROUBLED ABOUT THE FUTURE

In the first year of Belshazzar king of Babylon, Daniel
had a dream and visions of his head while on his bed.
Then he wrote down the dream, telling the main facts.

DANIEL 7:1 NKJV

The tables are turned: Daniel is the one dreaming now. And the **interpretation** is troubling. Verse 28 tells us that he kept the matter to **himself.**

I've had a few dreams that terrified me. I can still remember a **couple** of nightmares from my childhood—they seem silly now but were **very frightening** then. As an adult, I've had dreams about my family being **persecuted,** my children being killed, and myself in terrible circumstances **after** I've made some horrible, sinful choices. I love the wonderful **wave of relief** in the morning when I realize it was "only a dream."

Not so for Daniel. He knew, at some point when God's timing **was right,** that his dream was going to come true. This may explain why **God rarely gives us a** heads-up about the future: the angst that comes **with knowing** is too upsetting. Occasionally, He trusts a few stalwart **ones like Daniel** with that kind of knowledge. But **probably** not us. Let's just **relax and** entrust the future to Him.

. . . .

Father, You know all, and I don't—and I think
that's a good thing. Amen and good night.

JOSEPH: PROTECTOR OF THE CHRIST CHILD

Then Joseph her husband, being a just man, and not wanting to make her a public example, was minded to put her away secretly. But while he thought about these things, behold, an angel of the Lord appeared to him in a dream, saying, "Joseph, son of David, do not be afraid to take to you Mary your wife, for that which is conceived in her is of the Holy Spirit. And she will bring forth a Son, and you shall call His name JESUS, for He will save His people from their sins." ... Now when they had departed, behold, an angel of the Lord appeared to Joseph in a dream, saying, "Arise, take the young Child and His mother, flee to Egypt, and stay there until I bring you word; for Herod will seek the young Child to destroy Him." When he arose, he took the young Child and His mother by night and departed for Egypt.

MATTHEW 1:19–21; 2:13–14 NKJV

What a special man this New Testament Joseph must have been!

He was asked to play a supporting role in a much larger story. He was probably the subject of gossip for years. He had to trade the simple life of a carpenter for one of drama and danger. He was commissioned to be protector of the infant Christ! God used dreams to guide Joseph in this challenging assignment.

We too have duties to fulfill, and they're not always easy. But even if God's ways of communicating have changed, He hasn't. He is always with us to strengthen and guide.

. . . .

Heavenly Father, like Joseph, let me accept whatever assignment You have for me tomorrow. And let me be willing, whatever the cost to me. Amen.

THE MAGI: STAR-FOLLOWERS

*Now after Jesus was born in Bethlehem of Judea in the days of
Herod the king, behold, wise men from the east came to Jerusalem,
saying, "Where is he who has been born king of the Jews? For we saw
his star when it rose and have come to worship him." . . . When they saw
the star, they rejoiced exceedingly with great joy. And going into the
house, they saw the child with Mary his mother, and they fell down and
worshiped him. Then, opening their treasures, they offered him gifts,
gold and frankincense and myrrh. And being warned in a dream not to
return to Herod, they departed to their own country by another way.*

MATTHEW 2:1–2, 10–12 ESV

The Magi were men who followed the patterns of the stars. God put the
message of Jesus' birth in the heavens, and the "wise men," as we commonly
call them, followed it to Bethlehem. Being from the East, a place steeped
in mysticism, they were firm believers in dreams. So after they visited
young Jesus, God used a dream to warn them not to return to Jerusalem,
where they would again encounter the suspicious Herod.

God rarely uses stars or dreams in our lives. But He does want to give
us direction and warning. They come through His Word and His Holy
Spirit. Let's make sure we're attentive to both.

· ·

*Lord, speak to me through Your Word, and guide me with
Your Spirit. Tomorrow, I want to follow You. Amen.*

PILATE'S WIFE:
CONCERNED SPOUSE

Now the governor's custom was to release one Jewish prisoner each year during the Passover celebration—anyone they wanted. This year there was a particularly notorious criminal in jail named Barabbas, and as the crowds gathered before Pilate's house that morning he asked them, "Which shall I release to you—Barabbas, or Jesus your Messiah?" Just then, as he was presiding over the court, Pilate's wife sent him this message: "Leave that good man alone; for I had a terrible nightmare concerning him last night."

MATTHEW 27:15–17, 19 TLB

Old wisdom says that men should listen to their wives.

Pilate should have heeded his wife when she interrupted him at work with an important message. Maybe she had a lot of dreams. Maybe he rolled his eyes and thought, *Another one?* But this must have been a particularly significant dream to have made her try to change his mind.

I wonder what the dream was. What did she foresee? The destruction of Jerusalem? The Holocaust? The horrors of hell? Did she understand that her husband was actually going to pass sentence on the King of kings?

Pilate didn't listen. He let public opinion and political pressure pull him into the tragic vortex of Jesus' crucifixion. But even through the governor's terrible choice, God was working out the salvation of all who would follow Jesus. Rest comfortably tonight under that wisdom and power.

. . . .

God, let me listen to the counsel of others I trust so my decisions tomorrow will not have tragic consequences. Amen.

JOB: MISERABLE DREAMER

"Am I the sea, or a sea monster, that you set a guard over me?
When I say, 'My bed will comfort me, my couch will ease my complaint,'
then you scare me with dreams and terrify me with visions, so that
I would choose strangling and death rather than my bones."

JOB 7:12–15 ESV

Job endured a lot. But God knew he could take it, and He was **with Job in his** tragedies.

Job talked with (or at) God through the whole process. Some **of what he had** to say wasn't mild—in these verses, he seems irritated **with the God of** heaven. Job complains that even when he hopes for relief in **sleep, he has** nightmares that frighten him.

Being from his particular time and place, Job may have had a **mystical leaning.** He seems to assume that these bad dreams are from God, **which may simply** be another form of testing. It is possible that Satan **was the author of** Job's nightmares. God did give the enemy permission to **"touch" Job in** any way, without actually killing him. Certainly, **torture of the mind—even** the sleeping mind—would fit Satan's diabolical **strategy.**

Even today, the devil will try to infiltrate our thoughts, **especially at** night. But "he who is in you is **greater** than he who is in **the world"** (1 John 4:4 ESV). And God's peace will "guard your hearts and your minds in Christ Jesus" (Philippians 4:7 ESV).

. . . .

Lord, tonight while I sleep, I turn my mind over to
You. Keep me safe from the enemy. Amen.

Section 8:
VISIONS IN THE BIBLE

ABRAM–VISIONS AND COVENANTS

"Look now toward heaven, and count the stars if you are able to number them." And He said to him, "So shall your descendants be." And he believed in the Lord, and He accounted it to him for righteousness.
GENESIS 15:5–6 NKJV

God appeared to Abram in a vision not only to promise him a flesh-and-blood heir but also to establish a covenant binding Abram and God for generations to come.

Abram lived long before the Bible was completed or the Holy Spirit had been sent to indwell believers. Back then, God spoke in more visible ways. People responded by sacrificing animals, a picture of Jesus' death that would one day pay the final atonement.

Abram, a man from a pagan culture, had a heart that sought after the Lord Jehovah. And God counted Abram's belief as righteousness. Through this man's family line, God blessed the world by sending Jesus as the perfect sacrifice.

God wants to establish His covenant with you too. Jesus' sacrifice is still effective. Tonight, as you lay down to sleep, believe in the Lord and be counted as righteous.

. . . .

Lord, tonight I ask You to accept my surrender and include me in Your covenant. In Jesus' name, amen.

SAMUEL: ANSWERING THE VISION

Now the boy Samuel was ministering to the LORD in the presence of Eli. And the word of the LORD was rare in those days; there was no frequent vision. At that time Eli, whose eyesight had begun to grow dim so that he could not see, was lying down in his own place. The lamp of God had not yet gone out, and Samuel was lying down in the temple of the LORD, where the ark of God was. . . . And the LORD called Samuel again the third time. And he arose and went to Eli and said, "Here I am, for you called me." Then Eli perceived that the LORD was calling the boy. Therefore Eli said to Samuel, "Go, lie down, and if he calls you, you shall say, 'Speak, LORD, for your servant hears.'" So Samuel went and lay down in his place. And the LORD came and stood, calling as at other times, "Samuel! Samuel!" And Samuel said, "Speak, for your servant hears." Then the LORD said to Samuel, "Behold, I am about to do a thing in Israel at which the two ears of everyone who hears it will tingle."

1 SAMUEL 3:1–3, 8–11 ESV

I'm guessing that none of us heard the audible voice of God when we were children. But Samuel did. God called to the boy in the quietness of the night. We're not told that he saw anything or felt anything—only that he heard the call.

Samuel was lying down, quiet before sleep, when God's voice came to him. Maybe our own quietness would also result in direction. Why not give it a try now?

. . . .

Father, let me hear Your voice—and let my answer be, "Speak, because I'm listening." Amen.

ANANIAS: VISION OF DISCIPLESHIP

*Now there was a disciple at Damascus named Ananias. The Lord said
to him in a vision, "Ananias." And he said, "Here I am, Lord." And the
Lord said to him, "Rise and go to the street called Straight, and at the
house of Judas look for a man of Tarsus named Saul, for behold, he is
praying, and he has seen in a vision a man named Ananias come in and
lay his hands on him so that he might regain his sight." But Ananias
answered, "Lord, I have heard from many about this man, how much
evil he has done to your saints at Jerusalem. And here he has authority
from the chief priests to bind all who call on your name." But the Lord
said to him, "Go, for he is a chosen instrument of mine to carry my
name before the Gentiles and kings and the children of Israel. For I
will show him how much he must suffer for the sake of my name."*

ACTS 9:10–16 ESV

Ananias was a man convinced of the authority of His Lord. When God told
him to mentor the terrorist and persecutor Saul of Tarsus, he obeyed.
We're not told that God reassured Ananias that he would be safe. But the
man went, and he was instrumental in discipling the new convert who
would become the great apostle Paul.

You may not have a vision about it, but this evening consider: Whom
would God like *you* to mentor?

. . . .

*God, I don't need a vision, but I do need Your direction.
Show me someone to mentor tomorrow. Amen.*

CORNELIUS: VISION OF DIRECTION

There was a certain man in Caesarea called Cornelius, a centurion of what was called the Italian Regiment, a devout man and one who feared God with all his household, who gave alms generously to the people, and prayed to God always. About the ninth hour of the day he saw clearly in a vision an angel of God coming in and saying to him, "Cornelius!" And when he observed him, he was afraid, and said, "What is it, lord?" So he said to him, "Your prayers and your alms have come up for a memorial before God. Now send men to Joppa, and send for Simon whose surname is Peter. He is lodging with Simon, a tanner, whose house is by the sea. He will tell you what you must do."

ACTS 10:1–6 NKJV

Cornelius was a man of battle—a Roman centurion. He dealt in concrete matters, the kind of things you could see and touch. But he was also a man with a reverence for God, a man who prayed and wanted to grow in his faith. God sent a vision of an angel to direct Cornelius to contact the apostle Peter.

God knows the real desires of our souls. And He always honors people who want to know Him better. Today we have many ways to grow that Cornelius lacked, so let's take full advantage of them. Your Bible is a great place to start.

. . . .

Father in heaven, lead me into a closer walk with You. And let it begin tonight. Amen.

PETER: VISION OF ENLIGHTENMENT

But Peter began and explained it to them in order: "I was in the city of Joppa praying, and in a trance I saw a vision, something like a great sheet descending, being let down from heaven by its four corners, and it came down to me. Looking at it closely, I observed animals and beasts of prey and reptiles and birds of the air. And I heard a voice saying to me, 'Rise, Peter; kill and eat.' But I said, 'By no means, Lord; for nothing common or unclean has ever entered my mouth.' But the voice answered a second time from heaven, 'What God has made clean, do not call common.' This happened three times, and all was drawn up again into heaven. And behold, at that very moment three men arrived at the house in which we were, sent to me from Caesarea."

ACTS 11:4–11 ESV

Peter was a devout Jew. Yes, he served Christ, but he was convinced of the rightness of the Jewish traditions and wary of admitting Gentiles into the fellowship. God knew He would have to convince Peter in a nontraditional way. He used food.

Now, maybe Peter loved to eat. Or maybe this was just a good illustration since the Jews had so many food laws. But God wanted Peter—and us—to know for sure that Jesus is available to any people group. As you slip off to sleep tonight, thank God that He included you.

. . . .

Father, help me to be open to the nuances of truth You want to show me. Amen.

PAUL: VISION OF CALLING

And a vision appeared to Paul in the night. A man of Macedonia stood and pleaded with him, saying, "Come over to Macedonia and help us." Now after he had seen the vision, immediately we sought to go to Macedonia, concluding that the Lord had called us to preach the gospel to them.

ACTS 16:9–10 NKJV

Paul has been called "the apostle to the Gentiles."

He came to Christ in an unorthodox way—a dramatic conversion on the road to Damascus. And he proceeded to live out an unusual life—preaching, teaching, tentmaking, writing, traveling, suffering, loving, and sacrificing. It was all necessary, he said, to be counted "worthy" of fellowship with his Lord.

When God told Paul through a vision to begin ministry to the pagan nations, he obeyed. Yes, the Jews believed they were preferred above others. But Paul responded to the call and went.

Maybe God will reveal some unorthodox thing that He wants you to do. Maybe He has an unusual ministry, a unique place of service, a difficult person to whom you must witness. Ask Him about it tonight, and go to sleep awaiting His incredible leading.

. . . .

Lord, lead me. Show me what ministry paths You want for me tomorrow. Let me see all people through Your eyes. Amen.

JOHN: ISLAND VISIONS

I, John, both your brother and companion in the tribulation and kingdom and patience of Jesus Christ, was on the island that is called Patmos for the word of God and for the testimony of Jesus Christ. I was in the Spirit on the Lord's Day, and I heard behind me a loud voice, as of a trumpet, saying, "I am the Alpha and the Omega, the First and the Last," and, "What you see, write in a book and send it to the seven churches which are in Asia."

REVELATION 1:9–11 NKJV

A revelation is a supernatural disclosure to humans.

John the apostle had such an experience after he was banished to Patmos, a small island in the Aegean Sea. Sent there as punishment for following Christ, John received visions and messages from the Lord for the seven churches of Asia Minor—and for us today.

What John wrote, in addition to the inspired writings of Paul, Peter, Jude, and the other biblical authors, was collected over time into what is called the "canon" of scripture. And everything that God requires of us is in this written Word. We should be wary of those who claim to have new revelations today.

We will not receive a revelation like John did, but we can receive new understandings of what is already in God's Word. Perhaps even tonight.

. . . .

Lord, tonight as I read, open my eyes to a deeper understanding of the truth in Your Word. Amen.

Section 9:
MIDNIGHT HAPPENINGS
MIDNIGHT IS FOR PRAISING

At midnight I rise to praise you, because of your righteous rules.
PSALM 119:62 ESV

Really? When you get up in the middle of the night for a drink **of water or to** use the restroom, you should also give praise? That's what the **psalmist says.**

To **be** honest, I rarely get up in the middle of the night—though **women** in a **different** season of life tell me that will change! If I do **get up in the** **wee hours,** I'm usually groggy and want to hurry back to my **bed as soon** **as possible.**

But it wouldn't hurt **me to** say a quick "thank you" for that **bed and this** house and—most of all—for Jesus, the Redeemer and Giver **and Sustainer.** One commentator mentioned that midnight, as the end **of one day and** the beginning of another, is a natural moment in which to offer praise.

Some people are up late doing jobs, feeding an infant, or providing care at an elderly person's bedside—and it would be a great idea to develop the habit of offering praise at midnight. Whatever the reason, if we're awake, let's think about giving praise. Nothing arduous, just a short and simple word of thanks to God.

* * *

Lord, I praise You in this midnight hour. Thank You
for the day past and the one beginning. Amen.

MIDNIGHT: THE PASSOVER

*At midnight the LORD struck down all the firstborn in the land of Egypt,
from the firstborn of Pharaoh who sat on his throne to the firstborn
of the captive who was in the dungeon, and all the firstborn of the
livestock. And Pharaoh rose up in the night, he and all his servants and
all the Egyptians. And there was a great cry in Egypt, for there was not
a house where someone was not dead. Then he summoned Moses and
Aaron by night and said, "Up, go out from among my people, both you
and the people of Israel; and go, serve the LORD, as you have said."*

EXODUS 12:29–31 ESV

I hope you and I never experience something like the first Passover—at least from the Egyptian perspective. How horrible for the firstborn to die at midnight! To think of someone from every family in the nation dying!

But to experience that Passover from the side of God's people would have been incredible. Imagine offering a sacrifice from your flock and splashing the blood on the front doorposts of your home. Think of gathering your children to explain the significance of the event and then eating a meal together as God commanded. Consider the awesome realization that you and your family are safe—covered by the blood—while people around you perish.

Be grateful tonight for God's salvation. And pray for opportunities to share it with others.

. . . .

*Lord God, the blood of Your Son, Jesus, rescues me from the power of
death, not just at midnight, but every minute of my life. Thank You. Amen.*

MIDNIGHT: WEIGHT LIFTING

*The Gazites were told, "Samson has come here." And they surrounded
the place and set an ambush for him all night at the gate of the city.
They kept quiet all night, saying, "Let us wait till the light of the morning;
then we will kill him." But Samson lay till midnight, and at midnight
he arose and took hold of the doors of the gate of the city and the two
posts, and pulled them up, bar and all, and put them on his shoulders
and carried them to the top of the hill that is in front of Hebron.*

JUDGES 16:2–3 ESV

I'm not fond of weight training in broad daylight. Weight training at midnight would have to be worse! But not for Samson. He was a very flawed man, but chosen by God to deliver the Israelites from their enemies. The Lord gave Samson miraculous strength for the job.

In this midnight occurrence, Samson was visiting a woman he should have avoided—and he became the target of a planned morning ambush. But not to worry: he laid quietly until midnight, before making off with the entire gate of the city.

I don't know what is lying in ambush for you tonight, but the God who gave Samson his strength has power for you too.

. . . .

*Father, midnight or noonday, I need Your strength
to defeat my enemy. In Jesus' name, amen.*

MIDNIGHT: THE LORD'S RETURN

"Be on guard, keep awake. For you do not know when the time will come. It is like a man going on a journey, when he leaves home and puts his servants in charge, each with his work, and commands the doorkeeper to stay awake. Therefore stay awake—for you do not know when the master of the house will come, in the evening, or at midnight, or when the rooster crows, or in the morning—lest he come suddenly and find you asleep."

MARK 13:33–36 ESV

One day, Jesus is coming back. But we don't know exactly when.

It seems that Christians used to talk more about this. But it is still a planned event, and it will take place when God says the time is right. Jesus told His followers that not even He knew the day and hour. The Father holds all the details in His keeping.

The apostle Peter wrote of scoffers who reject the idea of Jesus' second coming. They say, "Where is the promise of his coming? For ever since the fathers fell asleep, all things are continuing as they were from the beginning of creation" (2 Peter 3:4 ESV). Peter attributed the delay to God's patience—His desire for more people to accept His salvation. But God won't wait forever.

Or, as Jesus was saying, it could be at any time. Be ready!

. . . .

Lord Jesus, You might return at midnight tonight. I want to be ready and watching in a spiritual sense. In Your name I pray, amen.

MIDNIGHT: TIME TO BORROW

Then, teaching them more about prayer, he used this illustration:
"Suppose you went to a friend's house at midnight, wanting to
borrow three loaves of bread. You would shout up to him, 'A friend
of mine has just arrived for a visit and I've nothing to give him to
eat.' He would call down from his bedroom, 'Please don't ask me to
get up. The door is locked for the night and we are all in bed. I just
can't help you this time.' But I'll tell you this—though he won't do
it as a friend, if you keep knocking long enough, he will get up and
give you everything you want—just because of your persistence."
LUKE 11:5–8 TLB

It would have to be a very good friend, right?

If I went to a friend's home at midnight, yelling at her to let me borrow bread, it wouldn't be good. But this story is from a different culture with different rules.

Still, the friend is reluctant. Who wouldn't be? "Come on!" we'd say. "Everything is locked up. We're all in bed. Can't you wait until morning?" But then loyalty or guilt or just a desire to get rid of the late-night visitor kicks in.

Maybe though this story isn't really about getting bread from a friend. Maybe it's really a reminder that if you need something from God at midnight, He's never reluctant to give it. And. . .He's always awake.

- -

Lord, You let me come to You with my needs at any time
of day. Thank You for always listening. Amen.

MIDNIGHT: PRAISE SERVICE IN JAIL

A mob was quickly formed against Paul and Silas, and the judges
ordered them stripped and beaten with wooden whips. Again
and again the rods slashed down across their bared backs; and
afterwards they were thrown into prison. The jailer was threatened
with death if they escaped, so he took no chances, but put them into
the inner dungeon and clamped their feet into the stocks. Around
midnight, as Paul and Silas were praying and singing hymns to the
Lord—and the other prisoners were listening—suddenly there was
a great earthquake; the prison was shaken to its foundations, all
the doors flew open—and the chains of every prisoner fell off!
ACTS 16:22–26 TLB

Imagine it's midnight and you're in prison. Even worse, you can't move
from the spot you're in. Your back, beaten with rods earlier in the day, is
painful and bleeding. What are you going to do?

Cry, perhaps. Probably complain. Or maybe groan. But not Paul and
Silas.

These men were just as human as you and I. They felt the pain—
physical and emotional—just like anyone else would. But they made a
choice to praise God, in spite of their circumstances.

I can't say what's happening to you tonight, but I'm pretty sure it won't
be as bad as what Paul and Silas faced. If they could make the choice to
praise, so can you. So can I. And who knows what victories will come from it?

. . . .

Lord, I will praise You tonight even though everything isn't
perfect. You are great and worthy to be praised. Amen.

Section 10:

BEDTIME PRAYERS, PRAISES, AND PATTERNS

THE MORNING STAR

But when you consider the wonderful truth of the prophets'
words, then the light will dawn in your souls and Christ
the Morning Star will shine in your hearts.

2 PETER 1:19 TLB

Ancient Greeks called the morning star *Phosphorus*. The name had to do with "light-bringing," and since this celestial body is seen shining brightly in the east just before dawn, the name is appropriate. Today we know it as the planet Venus. Except for the sun and moon, it is brighter than any other object in the sky.

No doubt, the apostle Peter knew that this star was significant to the ancient mind. So he used it as a metaphor to illustrate the brilliant light Christ would shine into the hearts of those who know Him.

You're probably reading this at night, when the morning star isn't as obvious. But it's comforting to know that the light of Jesus is as steady and sure as Venus's appearance in the morning, right before dawn. If you have the Lord's constant light, you don't need to fear any darkness in your life. Praise Him for that right now.

. . . .

Father God, thank You for the light You brought to the world at
creation and for the light You gave the world in Your Son. I want Him
to shine brightly in my heart and then through me to others. Amen.

SHIELD ME

For You, O LORD, will bless the righteous;
with favor You will surround him as with a shield.

PSALM 5:12 NKJV

David was a man of battle. From his early days, warding off lions and bears trying to attack his sheep, to his slaying of the giant Goliath, to his years as king when he led troops into battle against God's enemies, David was a warrior.

Many of his psalms reflect a knowledge of weaponry and armor, just as many use battle language to describe situations. In today's verse, David acknowledges that God surrounds His people with favor, just like a shield. Shields were moved from side to side, to defend against attack from any direction and hide warriors from danger. In Ephesians 6:16, the apostle Paul admonishes Christians to take up the "shield of faith" to quench Satan's fiery darts. What a wonderful mental image to think God's favor surrounds *us* like that!

Whatever battle you face today, the God who surrounded David like a shield will surround you too. Just ask.

. . . .

God my Father, Your Word is true and for every generation.
Tonight, I ask You to be my shield, to protect me from Satan's schemes,
and to surround me with Your favor. Teach me to use the shield of
faith so I might be victorious tomorrow. In Jesus' name, amen.

YOU LOVE SMALL THINGS

*When I consider Your heavens, the work of Your fingers, the moon
and the stars, which You have ordained, what is man that You
are mindful of him, and the son of man that You visit him?*

PSALM 8:3–4 NKJV

David was not only a warrior; he was a musician. In fact, 2 **Samuel 23:1**
(NKJV) proclaims him the "sweet psalmist of Israel." The words **of Psalm
8, a** magnificent hymn of praise to the Creator, demonstrate his **inspired
poetic** mind.

In considering the vastness of the heavens and the beauty of the **stars,**
David asked, "What is man?" The obvious answer: not much **compared
to space.** But God loves His creation. He loves humankind. He loves **the
small,** insignificant people we are. He longs to be in relationship **with us.**
Yes, **the** God who created the Milky Way in the night sky feels joy **when I
want to** talk to Him.

Whatever is going on in your life tonight, the scene above **your head is
a constant reminder** of God. Join in the chorus of praise!

. . . .

*Oh Lord, I am nothing compared to You, but You love me and call me
significant because I am made in Your image—and because You gave
Your Son to redeem me. Tonight, I praise Your greatness! Amen.*

PRESERVE ME

Preserve me, O God, for in You I put my trust. O my soul, you have said
to the LORD, "You are my Lord, my goodness is nothing apart from You."
PSALM 16:1–2 NKJV

Not all of us face the physical danger that David often did—but all of us need preservation.

There are many things that would spoil or destroy us. Satan is never short of ideas for making us stumble. But God is greater, and nothing can touch us if we trust Him and commit to following Him.

The idea of *preservation* speaks to the laying up, the guarding, or the careful keeping of something precious. A "game preserve" is a place where wildlife is protected. A jar of "preserves" contains luscious fruit kept edible by sugar and a canning process. A "life preserver" is a flotation device meant to protect a person in dangerous waters.

Tonight, ask God to preserve you from evil. Trust in the Lord and in His power.

. . . .

Lord, by Your grace and power, preserve me tonight.
Even while I sleep, watch over me. In Jesus' name, amen.

YOUR FACE AND LIKENESS

As for me, I will see Your face in righteousness;
I shall be satisfied when I awake in Your likeness.
PSALM 17:15 NKJV

I am not usually thrilled with my face when I wake up in the morning. How about you?

Something about looking in the mirror reminds us of how old we are—and how much different we look when our hair isn't done and our skin has that "leftover from the night before" look.

The psalmist, however, has a good point: the "face" of God will always satisfy and delight us. Now, Jesus—who is God in bodily form—has a face, but God the Father does not. Jesus Himself told us the Father is Spirit (see John 4:24). So what does this verse mean?

Scripture often uses earthly terms to help us understand spiritual things—it speaks of God's eyes, His ears, and His strong right arm, for example. These words and phrases are meant to convey things about God's attributes so we can better understand Him. So this reference to God's "face" probably indicates His presence. The waking up here doesn't mean getting out of bed in the morning, but arising from the sleep of death to be alive for eternity.

God's presence will definitely delight us in that moment.

- -

Lord, Your presence is my goal. When I wake up tomorrow, help me
to follow You so I can be "awake" with You for all eternity. Amen.

YOU ARE WORTHY

I will call upon the LORD, who is worthy to be praised;
so shall I be saved from my enemies.
PSALM 18:3 NKJV

The word *worship* comes from the Old English "worth-ship."

This should be our focus when we think of praise to God. He is ultimately "worthy" to be "worshipped"—and He is the only One. This is not a narcissistic thing on His part, nor is it a fabrication of codependent followers. It is simply true.

We worship God because:

- He is the only eternal One—that sets Him apart from all others.

- He is the God of the living—everyone who follows Him is still living, on earth or in heaven.

- He is the God who died—no other religion has a deity who died in the people's place.

- He has given His Word—no other sect or creed has a testament like the Bible.

- He is the I AM—He has revealed Himself to us, and by faith we see that He is true.

Not only does God deserve our praise; He also rewards our praise by rescuing us—sometimes from our earthly troubles but always from our eternal ones.

Tonight, call on this "worthy" God. Give Him praise before you sleep.

. . . .

God, You are worthy of praise for so many reasons.
Tonight, I look up in honor of Your greatness. Amen.

LIKE DEER IN THE MOUNTAINS

It is God who arms me with strength, and makes my way perfect.
He makes my feet like the feet of deer, and sets me on my high places.
PSALM 18:32–33 NKJV

You'll find white-tailed deer throughout much of the United States, Canada, and Mexico. Other types of deer are native to Europe, Asia, and parts of the Middle East. Africa has its own unique type, the Barbary stag.

Throughout human history, deer have been seen as a symbol of grace and dignity—as beautiful, fleet, and harmless creatures. That seems to be the thought the psalm writer was sharing in today's scripture. The God we serve makes us like deer—sure-footed in the rocky places of life, able to ascend into the mountains of growth and blessing.

Tonight, keep this picture in your mind. Reject all thoughts of defeat. Keep climbing in the strength that God provides.

. . . .

Father God, thank You for giving me the courage to trust You
tonight. I want to climb the mountain in front of me tomorrow.
Please help me to do that. In Jesus' name, amen.

YOUR WORD IS AWESOME

The law of the Lord is perfect, converting the soul; the testimony of the Lord is sure, making wise the simple; the statutes of the Lord are right, rejoicing the heart; the commandment of the Lord is pure, enlightening the eyes; the fear of the Lord is clean, enduring forever; the judgments of the Lord are true and righteous altogether. More to be desired are they than gold, yea, than much fine gold; sweeter also than honey and the honeycomb. Moreover by them Your servant is warned, and in keeping them there is great reward.
PSALM 19:7–11 NKJV

Precious few things in this world can be labeled *perfect*.

Oh, sometimes we use the term because it seems to sum up something we really enjoy—a vacation spot, a wedding ceremony, a brand-new baby. Some things are so wonderful that, to our human minds, they seem like perfection. But, deep down, we know that nothing that originates in this world is truly perfect.

God's Word though is actually perfect. It is accurate and complete, lacking nothing. It shows us the way to a relationship with God. It tells the story of His love and the plan of redemption. It is our food and strength. It is sweet and rich. It warns us and rewards us. In a word, it's perfect!

Before you sleep tonight, thank God for this great gift.

. . . .

God, You've given me Your perfect Word. I'm thankful that by keeping it, I can be closer to You tomorrow than I am today. Amen.

GUIDE MY WORDS

Let the words of my mouth and the meditation of my heart be
acceptable in your sight, O LORD, my rock and my redeemer.
PSALM 19:14 ESV

If human beings didn't talk, it would be so much **easier to live a Christian** life.

At least, that's the way it seems. The New Testament book of James tells us that to control the tongue (our speech) is the greatest **form of self-control**. I would have to agree, wouldn't you? Sometimes the **most difficult** thing is *not* to say something—words of retort, self-defense, **pride, complaint**, or gossip.

God made us with the ability to verbalize our feelings. Since **we are** fallen by nature, that can be ugly. It takes His redeeming and **ongoing grace** to enable us to guard our words.

Did you have a problem with your words today? Did you say **something you shouldn't** have? Is there something you need to say that **you haven't?** Right now, before you go to sleep, determine to take care **of those words** as soon as you can tomorrow. Then pray this prayer from **your heart. . . .**

. . . .

Lord, I need Your power and grace for my speech. Help me to
control my tongue so that the words of my mouth and the thoughts
that come from my heart may be pleasing in Your sight. Amen.

I TRUST YOUR NAME

Some trust in chariots, and some in horses; but we
will remember the name of the LORD our God.
PSALM 20:7 NKJV

We trust brands, don't we?

Whether we're shopping for household appliances or toothpaste, we all rely on certain brand names to deliver the quality and service we need.

Now, any thrifty homemaker knows that it pays to bargain shop. Most of us are willing to "cheat" on some items—we'll buy the store brand or a generic version of something. But there are some pantry items for which I can't get away with a lesser brand. My family is particular about peanut butter and cereal and, yes, even toilet paper. So I buy off-brand items as I can but stick to the "real thing" on the important stuff.

The name of our God is the real thing—no generic version will do. Others may put their trust elsewhere (the psalmist listed chariots and horses, powerful symbols of a nation's might in those days), but we know that only God can give us what we need.

As you go to sleep tonight, praise God for His goodness—and for His "brand name" that can never be equaled.

. . . .

Father in heaven, Your name is the only one that
works. I praise Your name tonight. Amen.

WHY DO YOU FEEL SO FAR AWAY?

My God, My God, why have You forsaken Me? Why are You so far from helping Me, and from the words of My groaning? O My God, I cry in the daytime, but You do not hear; and in the night season, and am not silent.

PSALM 22:1–2 NKJV

I think all of us can identify with this prayer.

Some days, God and His grace and power seem distant, so far from our present reality. David knew about this. In Psalm 22, he expressed his anguish over crying out for the Lord by day and night but seeming to get no answer.

We know the truth: God is always near. And if we believe in Jesus, His Spirit actually lives inside us—that's pretty close. But sometimes we forget these truths due to the trauma we're enduring, or the stress that paralyzes our emotions, or the grief that threatens to overwhelm us.

Today's psalm is referred to as "messianic," meaning some of its descriptions fit happenings in the earthly life of Christ. We know that He felt forsaken on the cross, and He asked His Father why. If the Son of God experienced such human anguish, it is likely that we will also.

The truth, however, remains. And maybe tomorrow or the next day, our minds will balance out enough to embrace what our faith keeps telling us—God is there, all the time. And we can rest in that truth.

. . . .

Father, thank You for being near, even when my emotions are crazy. Amen.

THE WORLD IS YOURS

The earth is the Lord's, and the fullness of it, the world and
they who dwell in it. For He has founded it upon the seas
and established it upon the currents and the rivers.
PSALM 24:1–2 AMPC

Don't ever believe the lie.

You know, that lie about the world and everything in it (including us) coming from a series of chance events. Today's passage says the earth and the things and people that fill it belong to the Lord. He founded and established everything we know.

Evolution is a convenient theory for those who would like God to be absent from their worldview. Often, even Christians feel the pressure of "scientific evidence," as new theories are touted and new atheists arrive to challenge the Holy One and His Word.

But some things we know are true, despite any new claims. Eventually, the truth will win. The God who made this world will one day vindicate His name, revealing His power to the scoffers. For now though we will believe what He says, knowing that this world was made and is kept by Him.

Tomorrow, you will have some opportunity to prove that you believe in the Creator. Ask Him for wisdom to manage it well.

. . . .

Lord, the world is Yours. I am Yours. I sleep tonight
in this wonderful awareness. Amen.

LEAD ME

Show me the path where I should go, O Lord; point out the right road for me to walk. Lead me; teach me; for you are the God who gives me salvation. I have no hope except in you.

PSALM 25:4–5 TLB

Have you found that you like to do things on your own?

When my firstborn was small, she liked to say "Ashley do it" **whenever I helped** her with something. She was determined to be independent. **There were** times when that was appropriate and other times when I helped **her anyway.** I was Mom, and it was okay for me to still be the parent!

Sometimes, we're all like toddlers in God's eyes. We think we can **handle things on** our own. But we often discover we can't.

The psalmist realized that truth from the beginning. He laid out **a whole list of** needs: Show me what path to take. Point out the right road. **Teach me what** I need to know. There's no hope for me but You.

This is a good prayer for us to pray. We'll all need this attitude **tomorrow to keep ourselves** centered **and** humble and safe.

. . . .

Lord, I don't know everything. My knowledge is limited. Yours is not. Show me what I need to do and what decisions I need to make. Guide me tomorrow by Your Spirit. In Jesus' name, amen.

EXAM TIME

Examine me, O Lord, and prove me; try my mind and my heart. For Your lovingkindness is before my eyes, and I have walked in Your truth.
PSALM 26:2–3 NKJV

During my time in school, test day was never a favorite.

Though I was a good student, I was paranoid that I might have missed something in my study—or that I wouldn't remember what I *had* studied. But those exams are important for measuring our learning, for seeing if we really understand the concepts being taught.

It works the same way in the spiritual realm. And we, like David, should invite God to examine us. That takes courage. But it's better to be sure sooner rather than later whether we're "in the faith," as the apostle Paul wrote (2 Corinthians 13:5 NKJV).

The latter part of David's prayer though gives us reassurance. The lovingkindness (or favor) of our God is always observable—and because of it, we know that He will grant us mercy and grace as we walk in truth, knowing the condition of our hearts.

Before you close your eyes tonight, ask our loving God to examine and prove you.

. . . .

Lord, reveal to me anything in my heart that needs Your special work and grace. Help me to know the condition of my heart. Amen.

LIGHT FOR SALVATION

The Lord is my light and my salvation; whom shall I fear?
The Lord is the strength of my life; of whom shall I be afraid?
PSALM 27:1 NKJV

There are many things to fear at night.

Even if we've outgrown a fear of the dark, there are other things *in the dark* that can frighten us. Wild animals hunt at night. Most crimes happen at night. Many sins occur at night. Desperate people lose their inhibitions at night.

Isn't it amazing what light will do? It gives us reassurance and courage just by bringing illumination to our surroundings.

The psalm writer says that the Lord is "light," "salvation," and "strength." Because of that, he doesn't need to be afraid.

What is dark in your world this evening?

Your marriage?

Your job?

Your habits?

Your attitude?

Bring your trouble to the light, and surrender it to the Lord.

. . . .

Father, I need Your light for my situation. I thank You
for grace and strength. In Jesus' name, amen.

PRAISE FOR THE GENERATIONS

One generation passes away, and another generation comes;
but the earth abides forever. The sun also rises, and the sun
goes down, and hastens to the place where it arose.
ECCLESIASTES 1:4–5 NKJV

Don't you love those generational photos you see on social media?

A newborn with a proud daddy or mommy, and a grandparent, and a great-grandparent. Sometimes you can see the family resemblance throughout the group. It's a wonderful thing to be able to capture so much love in one place.

Yet we know that every person in that picture will eventually pass from the scene. The law of the earth is that one generation passes away and another takes its place. Cemeteries bear testament to the fact that no one lives forever. Even the calendar illustrates this fact—as the sun rises and sets, days, weeks, months, and years come and go. It's the same kind of cycle that takes place in our families.

The Lord Jehovah, however, is constant. He remains, unchanged and unchanging, through every generational cycle. Tonight, as you say your last prayers, thank Him for His constancy.

. . . .

Father in heaven, generations come and generations go. You are
faithful to every one of them, and You are faithful to me. Amen.

WHATEVER GOD DOES

I know that whatever God does, it shall be forever.
Nothing can be added to it, and nothing taken from it.
God does it, that men should fear before Him.
ECCLESIASTES 3:14 NKJV

God is active. He is always doing something good in the lives of those who know Him. And what He does lasts forever.

If you're like me, you like to look back over a day and bask in your accomplishments. Checking things off my to-do list gives me a sense of purpose and well-being. But I know that many of those things will have to be done again.

Laundry? Yes.

Cleaning? Of course.

Cooking? Check.

Watering flowers? Uh-huh.

Going through email? Absolutely.

And the list goes on and on.

These tasks are just part of living in our world. They have to be done over and over. They are not one-time events.

But it's not that way with God. Whatever He does lasts. No need for a repeat. No need to keep a list in case He forgets. He just does things that last for eternity.

. . . .

Lord, thank You for doing things permanently.
I want to love You more. Amen.

MADE FOR MORE

All go to one place: all are from the dust, and all return to dust.
Who knows the spirit of the sons of men, which goes upward,
and the spirit of the animal, which goes down to the earth?

ECCLESIASTES 3:20–21 NKJV

Animals are wonderful creatures of God. Many are intelligent, **responsive, fun, and lovable. But** they are not people.

These verses from Ecclesiastes illustrate that the human soul **ascends to God when death occurs.** There the soul is judged based on its **response to Christ while on earth.** And then the soul, the core of the person, **is sent either to eternal joy or** eternal punishment.

But animals have no souls. When verse 21 says the spirit of animals "**goes down to the earth,**" it means that there is no upward, eternal **journey of the soul to God.** We have to keep all this in proper context of **course: we humans were made to be** different from our pets and the wild **animals we find so compelling.** We were made for more!

It's good to know that in a world teeming with life, we are **special to God. So special** that He sent His own Son to die for our sins. **That thought should give us** great peace tonight.

. . . .

Lord God, I thank You for the animals and the joy they bring. But I thank You more for helping us understand Your work in humans. Amen.

I NEED DIRECTION

*Trust in the LORD with all your heart, and lean not on
your own understanding; in all your ways acknowledge
Him, and He shall direct your paths.*
PROVERBS 3:5–6 NKJV

When nighttime falls, decisions can weigh heavy on the mind. If you're like me, you've had nights when you hated going to sleep because you didn't want the morning to come.

God doesn't want us to dread any of the days He gives us. Instead, He wants us to trust Him with them, leaning on His wisdom to handle each one.

The writer of Proverbs admonishes us to trust in the Lord with *all of our* heart. And he tells us not to lean on any bit of our understanding without the filter of God's Word and His Spirit. We can't see every angle of a circumstance, but He does. We can't see the long-range outcome, but He can. We do not have His knowledge or the vantage point of eternity. So He wants us to ask for His guidance.

Tonight, in your last few minutes before falling asleep, turn your dread over to God. Ask for His wisdom to take the next day step by step. And just watch what He does.

. . . .

*Lord, You are wise and full of truth. Lead me in the way
I should go tomorrow. In Jesus' name. Amen.*

THAT SHINING PATH

But the path of the just is like the shining sun,
that shines ever brighter unto the perfect day.
PROVERBS 4:18 NKJV

"The best is yet to come." The saying is becoming my new favorite.

Though my temperament leans toward sentiment and retrospect, making the past seem to shine more beautifully than the present, God's Word says otherwise. The path of the just—those who have been redeemed and made right—gets brighter and brighter. Our future is better than our past. Heaven and eternity with Jesus are before us. It doesn't get much better than that.

As women, we cherish certain moments in our relationships. We might think back to the days of young romance or to new babies and growing children, becoming wistful for the emotion of those times. It's only human to do so.

But God says, essentially, "Yes, I've given you wonderful moments already, but I've got so many more—things you've never even dreamed of—just waiting for the right time." If we trust Him with the now and with the days to come, He will keep leading us in His bright paths.

If the blues are calling you tonight, don't give in. The path He's leading you on is brilliant with light yet to come!

. . . .

Father, thank You for giving me a future and a hope.
I can't wait to see what lies ahead in my bright path! Amen.

STAYING CENTERED

Ponder the path of your feet, and let all your ways be established.
Do not turn to the right or the left; remove your foot from evil.
PROVERBS 4:26–27 NKJV

Balance is one of the most difficult things to achieve.

Humans are lamentably prone to excess. Think about it: politics, **sports, food,** leisure—all these areas of life can be pitfalls if we are not **balanced.**

Excess is obvious in situations like drunkenness or heavy debt. **But sometimes** our imbalances are hidden. Still, there is an inevitable **day of reckoning** when excess rules our lives.

Jesus, though, was perfectly balanced at all times. He never gave **in to a temptation** to overdo. And He was tempted just like we are, **according to Hebrews** 4:15. So He knows what it's like—and He's able to give **us the grace to** overcome.

Tomorrow will bring new opportunities to indulge the self, **but you and I are called** to practice restraint, to reach for balance. Let's ask **God tonight to keep us from turning** to the **right or** left, but rather to be **centered in Him.**

. . . .

God, You hold all the grace I need for tomorrow. I want to be balanced.
Help me to say no to the temptation to overindulge. In Jesus' name, amen.

MAKE WISE PLANS

Go to the ant, you sluggard! Consider her ways and be wise,
which, having no captain, overseer or ruler, provides her
supplies in the summer, and gathers her food in the harvest.
PROVERBS 6:6–8 NKJV

Having a plan helps you to succeed.

I can overplan, for sure, but if I underplan not much is **accomplished.**
We must not be slaves to our plans, but we should always have some kind
of action in mind.

God's Word holds up the ant as an example of diligence and wise
planning. She gathers her supplies and lays up food at harvesttime. She's
just a tiny creature, one that most of us probably discount in the grand
scheme of life. But God notices, and He applauds when the ant does what
it is created to do.

We should take a cue from the ant, by planning our work and working
the plan. If we have a mental outline for tomorrow, its responsibilities and
requirements will be less frightening. There may be interruptions and
adjustments, of course, but we can view them as God's special appointments. For now, let's ask for His wisdom and rest securely in His guidance.

. . . .

Father God, You created the ant and You created me.
Thank You for the examples You put in the natural world. Give me
the wisdom to plan my day for Your glory and my good. Amen.

FLOURISHING, NOT FOLDING

He who trusts in his riches will fall,
but the righteous will flourish like foliage.
PROVERBS 11:28 NKJV

The world's security, it seems, depends on Wall Street. But ours doesn't.

The daily numbers of the Dow Jones and NASDAQ are vital to the economic balance of the world. Those in the know follow the statistics to see what financial decisions they should make in days to come.

But God's Word reminds us that trusting in riches leads to ruin. Ultimately, our stock portfolios and bank accounts will not preserve our lives.

Righteous people have put value in the right thing—trust in the Lord. They still care about money as a means of providing for their needs. But they also know that if it is taken away, they still have a firm foundation in Christ.

As you go to sleep tonight, remind yourself that you are resting in the power of the One who owns everything in the world. You will flourish if you put stock in Him.

. . . .

Heavenly Father, all the wealth that has ever been
is really Yours. I trust You tonight to give me what I
need to tomorrow, as I follow Your will. Amen.

SOCIAL LIFE PRAYERS

Be with wise men and become wise. Be with evil men and become evil.
PROVERBS 13:20 TLB

You become like your friends.

It's an old adage, but still true. We pick up the values and habits of those with whom we associate. This probably works for our associations through social media too.

If you're like many people, one of the last things you do before bedtime is skim through everybody else's recent postings. Medical professionals advise against that, because the lighted screen and the discussion stimulate a mind we're trying to calm down, but most of us do it anyway. We want to see what's happening in the lives of those people we call friends.

Proverbs reminds us that if we hang around with wise people, we will become wise. So tonight, maybe it's time to reevaluate our connections on social media. It's not wrong to have friends who are not Christ-followers—Jesus Himself was called the "friend of sinners." But if we identify mainly with those who don't honor the Lord, we may grow more like them.

Okay, now shut down your phone and go to sleep!

. . . .

Lord, may I be aware of how my friends influence me.
Please guide me in choosing my future friends well. Amen.

EYES ALL AROUND

The eyes of the LORD are everywhere,
keeping watch on the wicked and the good.
PROVERBS 15:3 NIV

Since the invention of the surveillance camera, it is **possible for homes and** businesses to have "eyes all around." But there is nothing as **all-seeing as the** eyes of the Lord.

When crimes are committed, the feed from a surveillance **camera is invaluable** to law enforcement. The video footage from cameras in **stores,** banks, gas stations, and parking lots often provides great clues, from **the physical** description of the perpetrator to the kind of car he or she **was driving** to the presence of other people in the incident.

But there is a much better security system than that: the God of **heaven never** misses a single detail. He sees everything in brilliant color and **high definition.** His perfect vision never needs a replay because He gets **it right the first** time.

Tonight, as you slip under your covers, thank God that **His vision is better than** twenty-twenty. Then go to sleep knowing **that you're under** His watchful care.

. . . .

Father in heaven, I'm in awe of Your power—
including Your ability to see everything happening at once.
Because of this, You never lose track of me. Thank You. Amen.

WARRIOR SPIRIT

He who is slow to anger is better than the mighty,
and he who rules his spirit than he who takes a city.
PROVERBS 16:32 NKJV

It's become trendy to be loudly opinionated. God expects something different.

Often, at night, we rehash things that happened during the day. It's easy to feel slighted or become irritated in our marriages, homes, and workplaces when we feel others aren't respecting our dignity or viewpoint. When people aggravate us with their words or behavior, culture has no problem with throwing disgust and anger right back at them. Scripture, though, calls us to practice restraint, a kind of ruling power over the spirit.

The desire to put other people in their place is a self-centered one, built on a desire for vindication or affirmation. It is a mark of a godly warrior to keep one's spirit in check and refuse to utter angry words.

Proverbs says it takes more strength to control ourselves than to conquer a city. It's a big deal with God, so get a good night's rest ahead of tomorrow's battle.

. . . .

Lord, I need Your strength tomorrow so that I can
rule well my spirit. In Jesus' name, amen.

CHEERFUL HEART, GOOD SLEEP

A cheerful heart is good medicine, but a crushed spirit dries up the bones.
PROVERBS 17:22 NIV

Would you rather go to bed happy or sad?

I **suppose** there are some who would say sad, but **most of us would rather** climb into bed with a light heart—with a feeling of joy **about the day ahead.** The writer of this proverb says having that kind of **attitude is like** taking a helpful medicine.

Many people take medications at bedtime, whether vitamins, **sleeping pills, or** prescriptions for a health condition. These are good, but a **joyful heart is** better. It's been scientifically shown that laughter is a **boost to health.**

Maybe you could read a lighthearted book, watch a good clean **comedian, or enjoy** a funny home video. Give yourself a joy boost at the end of **the day.**

But don't forget God's blessings, which will cheer you too. Focus **on the little favors** He's done for you—they may be insignificant to **others, but they will** make you smile.

If God's Word recommends it, we should try it. Take **the medicine of a cheerful heart** tonight.

. . . .

Lord, thank You for laughter and fun. Tonight, I ask
You to help me cultivate a cheerful heart so it can be a
medicine to help me rest. In Jesus' name, amen.

LONGINGS FOR THE HERMIT LIFE

So I said, "Oh, that I had wings like a dove! I would fly away and be at rest. Indeed, I would wander far off, and remain in the wilderness."
PSALM 55:6–7 NKJV

When my brother was young, he would say he wanted to be a mountain man, to live alone in the wilderness.

Probably all of us have longed for something like that—for a day, maybe. There's something appealing about escaping from people and pressure and living in the pure freedom of nature. It speaks to the stressed and scheduled part of us.

But, to be honest, not all of us would thrive in that kind of life. There are drawbacks to isolation. While we could do with a bit less stress, running to the wilderness is probably not the answer.

Still, we understand what David meant in Psalm 55. If he could escape all the stuff happening in his life, he could be at rest. The idea of flying away like a dove to some peaceful corner was quite attractive to him. In our harried lives, it's attractive to us.

But usually we won't be able to do that. We must stay in the game, allowing our God to rest our souls and minds through His grace. And He will.

Besides, those wilderness beds aren't all that great anyway!

. . . .

Father God, tonight give me rest, and let my mind escape the pressure of the day. I rest in the freedom of Your grace. Amen.

FOR RANDOM FEARS

*Whenever I am afraid, I will trust in You. In God (I will praise His word),
in God I have put my trust; I will not fear. What can flesh do to me?*
PSALM 56:3–4 NKJV

Fear can attack at any time, but it loves the nighttime best.

When we can't see physically, we are often tormented **mentally**. **Fears
strike** us from all directions, and we can spend restless hours **miserable
because** of the dramatic imaginings in our minds. Sometimes **we feel
paralyzed,** unable to get on another train of thought.

The only surefire way of dealing with fear is to rely on the Author **of
peace.** The psalmist had learned this secret. He said that he was **going
to trust** in God "whenever" he was afraid. That means any time of **day or
night.** There is no mental anguish that God cannot calm.

My husband's grandmother was a slave to irrational fears. She **worried
about** things that would never happen, going through life **nervous and
unsettled.** That's a tough way to live, and God offers a way out.

Tonight, as you try to quiet your mind before bedtime, **give God your
fears and all** the imaginings of your active mind. And **remember that you
can** *trust* Him.

. . . .

*Heavenly Father, You can help me win this battle with
fear. Right now, I make a choice to trust You for one
second, and then for the next, and the next. Amen.*

BE EXALTED

Be exalted, O God, above the heavens; let Your glory be above all the earth.
PSALM 57:5 NKJV

God is always exalted. And His glory is above the earth in the night sky.

Many things exalt the name of our God. And there is something peculiarly spectacular about the expanse of the heavens with its star-dotted canvas. The New Testament letter to the church at Rome says specifically that people who see the beauty of creation become accountable to believing in the Creator (see Romans 1:20).

You are not doubting that tonight—you know that there is a Creator God who loves us and sent His Son to buy us back from the corruption of sin. You know that every single planet in the night sky is there because He decrees it. You know that though man has walked on the moon, there are galaxies beyond our vision and certainly beyond our reach. You know that God is infinite and even the vastness of space cannot hold Him.

So tonight, remind yourself of God's greatness. Then decide in your heart to honor Him tomorrow in all you do—so that His glory may be above all the earth.

. . . .

Creator God, Your majesty is beyond my comprehension. Help me to honor You so that through me, somehow, others might be directed to You. Amen.

WAKE UP!

Awake, my glory! Awake, lute and harp! I will awaken the dawn. I will praise You, O Lord, among the peoples; I will sing to You among the nations. For Your mercy reaches unto the heavens, and Your truth unto the clouds.
PSALM 57:8–10 NJKV

I don't like to wake up.

Since I resist going to bed in the first place, I have a difficult time getting out of bed in the morning. Had the psalmist been my neighbor, I might not have liked him—he was expressing loud praise to God on musical instruments, awakening the dawn!

Whatever time we get up, we can use our morning playlists to exalt God too. The start of day would be a lovely time for a hymn of praise, just as evening seems right for more reflective music. The soul is more open to the wonder of God at dawn and dusk, and music at these times can turn our attention more fully to the One who creates each day. As another psalm says, "Cause me to hear Your lovingkindness in the morning, for in You do I trust; cause me to know the way in which I should walk, for I lift up my soul to You" (Psalm 143:8 NKJV).

Tonight, as you set your alarm, remember that awakening with a word of praise will make all of tomorrow go better!

. . . .

Father, please wake me in the morning with a song in my heart and on my lips. Amen.

ROCK ME TO SLEEP

From the end of the earth I will cry to You, when my heart is overwhelmed; lead me to the rock that is higher than I. For You have been a shelter for me, a strong tower from the enemy. I will abide in Your tabernacle forever; I will trust in the shelter of Your wings.
PSALM 61:2–4 NKJV

Before my first child was born, I bought a rocking chair at a second-hand store.

I still have that chair. It brings back memories of sweet little ones, early morning feedings, and all the wonder of being a new mother. I sure enjoyed rocking my babies.

God wants to comfort us in His embrace, just as I did my little ones. He invites all of us to draw close to Him and lean into His strength. He doesn't have a chair that rocks, but He is *the* Rock.

When my children were tired at night, they would become grumpy and demand their mommy. I was their shelter until they fell asleep. In a much larger way, God is our shelter—our "strong tower," in fact—to keep us safe from the enemy all day and all night.

Are you grumpy tonight?

Overwhelmed?

In pain?

Abused?

Discouraged?

Come to the Rock of Ages. Find comfort in Him as you drift off to sleep.

Father God, I am needy tonight. Give me Your comfort and peace so I can sleep. Amen.

EVERY PART OF ME

Because Your lovingkindness is better than life, my lips shall praise You.
Thus I will bless You while I live; I will lift up my hands in Your name.
PSALM 63:3–4 NKJV

A life of praise is a whole-body experience.

When we surrender ourselves to God, we give Him everything. There is no reservation, no portion of our goals, gifts, personality, relationships, or future that we withhold. Neither can we reserve any part of our physical body. To belong to God is a complete surrender.

The writer of today's passage names lips and hands as tools for praising the Lord. But since we've been discussing rest in our time together, how about using sleep itself as a form of praise? As we relax in our beds, our physical bodies are actually praising God by submitting to the rest He gives. We praise Him by following His plan for us—and sleep is a part of that. Think of it: we praise God by praying, singing, serving others. . .and sleeping.

In the morning, when you awaken with renewed energy and inspiration, your body will praise God in its daylight cycle. For now, praise Him in the nighttime mode with the hours of rest He gives.

. . . .

Heavenly Father, let my whole physical experience
in this body be one of praise to You. Amen.

EARTH PRAISE

*O God who saves us. You are the only hope of all mankind throughout
the world and far away upon the sea. He formed the mountains by his
mighty strength. He quiets the raging oceans and all the world's clamor.
In the farthest corners of the earth the glorious acts of God shall startle
everyone. The dawn and sunset shout for joy! He waters the earth
to make it fertile. The rivers of God will not run dry! He prepares the
earth for his people and sends them rich harvests of grain. He waters
the furrows with abundant rain. Showers soften the earth, melting
the clods and causing seeds to sprout across the land. Then he crowns
it all with green, lush pastures in the wilderness; hillsides blossom
with joy. The pastures are filled with flocks of sheep, and the valleys
are carpeted with grain. All the world shouts with joy and sings.*

PSALM 65:5–13 TLB

You've heard of Earth Day. Did you know you that every day is "earth day"
in the spiritual realm?

Every single day this earth responds to its Creator and does what it's
supposed to do. Simply by being mountains and oceans and plains and
forests, the parts of creation all glorify the God of heaven. The dawn and
the sunset seem to shout joyfully just by happening each day! And then
God sends rains to make the green grass grow, He causes the fields to ripen
and the flocks and herds to multiply. The whole world sings God's praise.

Why don't you join in tonight?

*God, this is Your earth and Your night. I praise You
by being who You made me to be. Amen.*

A PRAYER FOR SHINING

God be merciful to us and bless us, and cause His face to shine upon us.

PSALM 67:1 NKJV

Like the sun that beams in the sky, God's face shines on those who put their trust in Him.

This ancient prayer is a petition for God to smile with **favor on the one who** prays, because a smiling face denotes benevolence and **blessing.**

To ask for God's smile:

- **we** need to be in relationship with Him
- **we** need to be at peace with Him
- **we** need to be at peace with those around us
- **we** need to have submissive hearts

God does not turn His smile on those who are rebelling against **Him. He does** not beam on those who do not want to love Him or His **people. Despite** popular sentiment, God does not bless people living **in known** sin. True, He will send a general blessing on the earth, as **Matthew 5:45** (NKJV) says: "He makes His sun rise on the evil and on the **good, and sends** rain on the just and on the unjust." But God gives specific **and wonderful** blessings to those who are called by His name.

It is night now, time for the moon and stars to shine. But, if you are God's, you can ask for Him to beam down on you too.

. . . .

Father, cause Your face to shine on me tonight; I am Yours. Amen.

SEA CREATURE PRAISE

Let heaven and earth praise Him, the seas and
everything that moves in them.
PSALM 69:34 NKJV

The deep parts of the ocean are dark. No light penetrates those hidden caverns and coves.

Beneath the shimmering ocean waves, sometimes miles below the surface, lies a wild and mysterious world. Exotic fish and scaly creatures inhabit this place the Creator designed. Odd and eerily beautiful formations glorify Him. Everything that occupies the ocean depths testifies to God's greatness.

In the deepest ocean, it is always night. There are places where no sun ray or diver's light has ever shone. Undisturbed since creation, these portions of the earth are dark, dark, dark. The living creatures in them sleep and wake in blackness.

Thankfully, you and I do not live that way. God created humankind to enjoy the cycles of day and night. So, while the deep sea praises Him tonight, never knowing anything but gloom, you can praise God for the bright morning to come.

. . . .

Lord of earth and sea, I praise You tonight in my bed while the
creatures You've made praise You from their habitats. Amen.

PRAISE FROM BIRTH

For You, O Lord, are my hope, my trust, O LORD, from my youth.
Upon you I have leaned from before my birth; you are he who took
me from my mother's womb. My praise is continually of you.

PSALM 71:5–6 ESV

Do you know what time of day you were born?

Babies come at all times of the day and night. Though cesarean **section** deliveries can be scheduled, only God can plan the exact **time of a natural** birth.

At the moment of our arrival, none of us were able to praise God—not consciously, at least. Infants do not have the cognitive skills for that. **But we all grow** in wisdom and stature, as Luke 2:52 says of Jesus, and we **begin to grasp** God's vital role in our lives. From the vantage point of **adulthood, we can** see how He has sustained our lives from the beginning.

Whether or not we've had the experience of giving birth, the **one thing we all have** in common is that we *were* born—in the sight of **the God who watches both** day and night. And as you go to sleep this night, **praise Him for the way** He has watched over you from the very **beginning. . . even** before you consciously knew Him.

. . . .

Father, I praise You for watching over me from the time of
my birth. I could not have lived without You. Amen.

PRAYER FOR REST IN OLD AGE

So even to old age and gray hairs, O God, do not
forsake me, until I proclaim your might to another
generation, your power to all those to come.
PSALM 71:18 ESV

For many people, sleep patterns change as they age. Babies typically sleep a lot, and toddlers need naps in the daytime. By the time we're teenagers, many of us prefer to stay up late and sleep in the next day—maybe until 1 p.m.!

As adults, most of us take on a "typical" schedule, working a daytime job and perhaps managing kids of our own, with their school and activity calendars. It's tiring work, and we appreciate the opportunity to rest each night.

But sometimes the stresses of family life interfere with that sleep—and as we grow even older and our kids move on, we find that we don't rest as well as we'd like to. The aging of our bodies, with its related health issues, can make finding a full night's sleep a challenge. In fact, old age brings with it many challenges, both physical and emotional.

That's why the psalmist prayed that God would not forsake him when he grew old. Even when he showed the signs of advanced years, he wanted to proclaim the Lord's might to the next generation.

We're all getting older, but we know that the God of heaven will be with us. There is no season of life in which He will not be present, day and night.

. . . .

Father God, be with me now and be with me when I am old.
I praise You for caring for me in every season of life. Amen.

FIGHTING INSOMNIA WITH PRAISE

In the day of my trouble I sought the Lord; my hand was stretched
out in the night without ceasing; my soul refused to be comforted.
I remembered God, and was troubled; I complained, and my spirit
was overwhelmed. Selah. You hold my eyelids open; I am so troubled
that I cannot speak. I have considered the days of old, the years of
ancient times. I call to remembrance my song in the night;
I meditate within my heart, and my spirit makes diligent search.

PSALM 77:2–6 NKJV

Insomnia is a result of sin in our world.

Really. If the world were perfect, we would have no difficulty falling asleep and getting the rest God designed our bodies to need. But since all the rhythms and cycles of our bodies and our environment have been skewed since the Fall, challenges like insomnia plague the human family.

Physicians and sleep centers can help determine the physical causes of sleeping problems—such as apnea, an issue with breathing. Other physiological issues can contribute as well, and there are medicines and techniques to address them.

But for those of us who just experience a restless night now and again, it's good to take the prescription of the psalmist. He called to mind comforting songs in the night; he meditated in his heart and diligently searched for ways to praise the Lord. Why not give that a try this evening?

. . . .

Lord God, tonight I turn my thoughts and meditations to You. Amen.

BEDTIME STORIES

For I will show you lessons from our history, stories handed down to
us from former generations. I will reveal these truths to you so that
you can describe these glorious deeds of Jehovah to your children
and tell them about the mighty miracles he did. For he gave his
laws to Israel and commanded our fathers to teach them to their
children, so that they in turn could teach their children too.

PSALM 78:2–6 TLB

Do you remember some favorite stories or books from your childhood?
Have you saved some of them in boxes or looked for them online? Many
parents love to share their old favorites with their children, handing down
stories to the next generation.

Most children like books at bedtime. The soothing tones of a parent's
voice, the adventures of the characters in an age-appropriate plot, and
the rhythmic cadence of language make this experience one that bonds
parents and children.

God knows the power of story. He created us to enjoy narrative, and
Jesus often told stories to share spiritual truths. Scripture says we should
"hand down" to our children the stories of God's great power in our lives
and the lives of others. Even if you don't have children of your own, there
are probably nieces, nephews, or neighbors you could benefit.

And you can always enjoy a classic story yourself in God's Word. There
are plenty to choose from tonight!

. . . .

Lord, thank You for recording Your mighty deeds
so I can read them tonight. Amen.

OUR SUN AND SHIELD

*For the L*ORD *God is a sun and shield; the L*ORD *will give grace and glory; no good thing will He withhold from those who walk uprightly.*

PSALM 84:11 NKJV

God is whatever we need.

Remember the stories in the Old Testament? When His people trusted in Him, God was the answer.

He was the substitute sacrifice for Isaac.

He was the dry path through the Red Sea.

He was the water from a desert rock.

He was the manna in the wilderness.

He was the insulation in the fiery furnace.

He was the muzzle on the lions' mouths.

And He is what *you* need tonight.

The psalmist says that the Lord is both a sun and a shield. He will shine on us and protect us. He knows what we need at any moment.

So what do you need tonight? Protection? Comfort? Peace? Guidance? Turn your needs into prayers to the One who is everything.

. . . .

Father, tonight hear my prayer as I tell You my need.
You have no limits, and I'm grateful. Amen.

A NIGHTTIME PRAYER
FOR FORGIVENESS

For You, Lord, are good, and ready to forgive,
and abundant in mercy to all those who call upon You.
PSALM 86:5 NKJV

Have you received God's forgiveness?

Those of us who grew up in the church are very familiar with **the teachings of the Bible** and the way of salvation. But sometimes this **familiarity can be detrimental. We** might assume we are believers without ever **having personally received God's** mercy for ourselves.

Forgiveness is a gift that can only come through the divine **enablement of God. He offers us** forgiveness because Jesus died in our place—and **His sacrifice is sufficient to** atone for any sin, no matter how horrible. **We can extend forgiveness to** others through His grace at work in us. **We can even forgive ourselves for the** failures that plague our memories.

Psalm 86 tells us that God is ready to forgive, and abundant in **mercy to all who call on Him.** Since He is absolute Truth and cannot lie, **we can take Him at His word.** We can have confidence in asking God **to hear and forgive us.**

If you have never asked Him to be your Savior, tonight **would be a wonderful time to** do that!

. . . .

God, I need forgiveness, and Your Word says You are ready
to offer it. So, right now, I ask You to forgive my sins because
of Jesus' death, and give me new life in Him. Amen.

IN HIS HANDS

The heavens are Yours, the earth also is Yours;
the world and all its fullness, You have founded them.
The north and the south, You have created them.

PSALM 89:11–12 NKJV

When my children were little, I taught them the song "He's Got the Whole World in His Hands." Remember that simple lyric? It's still true today.

The youngest children, with their literal way of thinking, no doubt have a mental image of God's really big hands actually holding the globe. But since God the Father has no physical body, this song really indicates that He can intervene in any way necessary for the continuation of the universe and the people in it.

The nouns in today's passage encompass everything—the heavens, the earth, "the world and all its fullness"—north and south, east and west. God is the founder and sustainer of the world. He made it and He keeps it going.

Atheists and evolutionists like to predict cataclysmic events, catastrophic endings to the world as we know it—they just can't acknowledge the One who upholds all things. But we know that nothing will happen tonight or tomorrow that God does not allow, and we can sleep soundly knowing that He does indeed have the whole world in His hands.

. . . .

Heavenly Father, the world is Yours,
and so am I. I rest in You tonight. Amen.

JUST LIKE ONE NIGHT

For a thousand years in Your sight are like yesterday when it is past, and like a watch in the night. You carry them away like a flood; they are like a sleep. In the morning they are like grass which grows up: in the morning it flourishes and grows up; in the evening it is cut down and withers.

PSALM 90:4–6 NKJV

"Just watching the grass grow." Have you ever heard someone say that? It's an expression that means things are happening slowly.

But the Bible uses a grass analogy more than once to describe the *brevity* of life on earth. The grass grows up, flourishing in the morning, only to be cut down by evening. From God's viewpoint, even the passing of years is but a moment.

God dwells outside of time, in eternity. There are no years, no past or present—everything to God is simply *now*. He created time for us, for this earth. So to Him a thousand years could be just yesterday—like a watch in the night.

I don't know how long this night seems to you. Sometimes, because of what's happening in our lives, nights can feel a thousand years long! But the Lord is with you. To Him, the longest night is only a moment.

. . . .

God, thank You for being timeless. Please watch over me this night. Amen.

NUMBERED NIGHTS

So teach us to number our days, that we may gain a heart of wisdom.
PSALM 90:12 NKJV

How many nights have you lived so far? For me, I have no idea. I suppose it would be simple enough to calculate, but God doesn't even have to do the math. He already knows. For me. For you. For your family. For your church congregation. For your county. For your state. For our country. For the world. That's right—He knows those details.

Why even consider such a question? The benefit to knowing how many nights we've spent on earth is realizing the inevitable passage of time—how quickly life goes by. This isn't meant to be morbid but rather a reality check. We all need that from time to time.

The psalmist says that considering our own life span helps us to develop a heart of wisdom. And that sounds like a great thing to me. It may not be terribly comforting to think that we're working through our allotted nights, but the upside is that eternity with the Lord has no measure. It is wise to prepare for that time.

. . . .

Lord, help me to think about my life—my days and nights—and let me spend all of it for You. Amen.

WHAT YOU'VE DONE TODAY

And let the beauty of the LORD our God be upon us, and establish the work of our hands for us; yes, establish the work of our hands.

PSALM 90:17 NKJV

I hate it when my work gets "undone." Know what I mean?

Work can be undone for many reasons—the kids make a mess on the counter, a storm knocks over the fence you built, a careless driver cuts through your front lawn. My mother has often remarked about the repetition of housework, the washing of the same dishes, the vacuuming of the same floors, the laundering of the same linens again and again. Of course, there is humdrum in other professions too, but the domestic scene does seem to have more than its share of tasks that must be endlessly repeated.

The prayer of Moses in Psalm 90 petitions the Lord to "establish" the work people do for Him. The service we render to God has far more staying power than anything we try to accomplish for ourselves. He knows how to make our efforts effective in the lives of others and in the advancement of His eternal purpose. Let Moses' prayer be yours tonight, as you think back on what you've done for God today.

. . . .

Father in heaven, may the work I've done in Your name outlast me and bring You glory. Amen.

THE DELIGHT OF COMFORT

In the multitude of my anxieties within me, Your comforts delight my soul.

PSALM 94:19 NKJV

Delight is a word used for luscious desserts as well as the emotion of a woman holding her newborn grandchild. It's a word with a variety of senses.

But probably nothing is as soothing as the delight of God's comfort to troubled spirits. Life is not only physical, but emotional, mental, and spiritual too. As humans, we are an integrated living system, susceptible to stress, fear, confusion, and pain. We are affected by the ongoing ebb and flow of family life, jobs, and the larger troubles of our world.

Anxiety is a ballooning phenomenon. Once it takes root, it grows, rising higher and higher in the mind until it blocks rational thought—even faith in God.

I don't know what anxieties you face tonight, but I'm sure you have some. For overwhelming anxiety, you may need to seek out a pastor or Christian counselor who can help you think through strategies to deal with it. But for the everyday, garden-variety stresses, God can bring His own comforts to you. In them, you can find delight again.

. . . .

Lord God, direct me to the comfort You want me to embrace—Your Word, another's counsel, a support group. I want to delight in You. Amen.

DEPTHS AND HEIGHTS

In His hand are the deep places of the earth; the heights of the hills are His also. The sea is His, for He made it; and His hands formed the dry land.
PSALM 95:4–5 NKJV

The Grand Canyon, the Royal Gorge, Death Valley. . .some of the deep places of the earth. Whether God formed them in the beginning or whether He used the cataclysmic forces of the great flood to do it, they are still of His design.

Generally, I don't like to think about being in deep places. Drowning is one of my fears, and "deep places" undoubtedly speak to that. Falling is a sensation that few of us like, and to tumble into a deep place is a horrible thing to consider.

When I was in college, the story of a little girl who fell into an abandoned well shaft made national news. The country held its breath for days while crews of rescue teams strategized and attempted over and over to get her out. When she was finally freed from that "deep place" and brought back up to her joyful family, the good news was broadcast to an eager audience.

Tonight, are you in a deep place? Or does this reading find you on a hill or mountaintop? God created both, and to Him, there is no difference. You are seen by God, and safe in His care.

. . . .

Father God, I rest in Your sight and in Your keeping. Amen.

SOOTHING SOUNDS

Let the field be joyful, and all that is in it.
Then all the trees of the woods will rejoice.

PSALM 96:12 NKJV

Do you like to sleep with noise? My husband does. "White noise" is his favorite way to block out the sounds of family life in the rest of the house. Some people sleep with a fan whirring. The hum of the car wheels on pavement puts many of us to sleep when we're traveling (and, hopefully, someone else is driving).

God put night noise into our world. Many birds become musical after dark—the owl and the whip-poor-will come alive in the nighttime hours. Crickets and cicadas chirp merrily in the night. Even inanimate things contribute to the symphony—the whisk of the breeze in the pine trees or the rustle of wind in the oak's leaves.

The psalm writer tells us that even the trees of the woods can rejoice. And I believe God gave them both daytime and nighttime repertoires. Tonight, as you prepare to sleep, why not listen for the music they make?

. . . .

Heavenly Father, thank You for night noise and
nature music. I'm listening tonight. Amen.

WATCH YOUR EYES

I will behave wisely in a perfect way. Oh, when will You come to me? I will walk within my house with a perfect heart. I will set nothing wicked before my eyes.
PSALM 101:2–3 NKJV

The eyes are our gatekeepers. What you intentionally focus on will have a tremendous impact on your behavior. David knew this, so he said, "I will set nothing wicked in front of me." Have you made that commitment?

People around the world have evening viewing habits—whether they watch a large screen in the front room or a small device in the bedroom. You may watch the news, catch a funny video clip, contemplate a TED talk, or just view your grandchildren on Facebook. But there are always other, more sinister options available. Satan makes sure of this. Wherever God has people, the enemy will be there to offer destructive alternatives.

Tonight, make the commitment King David did: don't put anything wicked before your eyes. Behave yourself in your house in a perfect way. If you make that choice, He will give you the strength to live it out.

. . . .

God my Father, give me the courage and strength to turn from wicked things as I choose what to set before my eyes. In Jesus' name, amen.

CLEAR CONSCIENCE

As far as the east is from the west, so far has He
removed our transgressions from us.
PSALM 103:12 NKJV

It's hard to sleep with a guilty conscience. The little voice in our mind that tells us we've wronged someone or offended God is really a gift to us. It is supposed to bring us back to Him, just like an illness brings a patient to the doctor.

The distance between east and west is unlimited, since you can keep going in either direction without ever reaching the end. God used this illustration to show us just how far away He puts the sins we confess to Him. It's a distance that cannot be calculated or understood—but a distance that brings us assurance and peace.

Tonight, if something is weighing heavily on your conscience, just give it to God in confession. Then resolve to make things right tomorrow. Finally, thank God for two things: first, that your conscience is working fine and, second, that east and west are so far apart!

. . . .

Father in heaven, I bring You my guilt tonight.
Cleanse me from this sin. I know You will remove it as far
as the east is from the west. In Jesus' name, amen.

HE KNOWS WE'RE DUST

For He knows our frame; He remembers that we are dust.
PSALM 103:14 NKJV

"Dust bunnies" aren't bunnies. They're little balls of hair, spiderwebs, dirt particles, and other household nasties that accumulate in corners and under furniture. Bunnies are cute. Dust, not so much.

To be brutally honest, we're just lumps of dust ourselves. That's what God formed us out of—the dirt, the earth, the habitat He made. Thankfully, we're held together by His breath while we're living. We don't disintegrate until we're in the cemetery.

Being dust means we are earthy in our perspective, with earthlike limitations and challenges. God, our Creator, knows this—and He keeps it in mind as He works on us through His Spirit.

Because we're simply dust, we're weak, we're winding down, we need sleep. God knows that. So tonight He's urging you to get some sleep, so you can find His better perspective on life in the morning. He knows our fragile "frame" very well.

. . . .

*Lord, I'm glad You know all about me. Please hold
me together with Your grace. Amen.*

THE NIGHT CREATURES

You make darkness, and it is night, in which all the beasts
of the forest creep about. The young lions roar after their
prey, and seek their food from God. When the sun rises,
they gather together and lie down in their dens.

PSALM 104:20–22 NKJV

I am not a fan of bats. They lurk in the dark of night, swooping **down from high** places to find their prey. I know they're seeking bugs, navigating **by a powerful** internal radar, but I don't want them anywhere near me.

God made certain creatures for the dark. First He made the **darkness, then He** crafted the animals to fit it. Their little internal clocks know **when dusk is** approaching, and they gear up for action.

Our verse for tonight relates how even in the hunt of nighttime **preda-tors, God** is the provider. He makes sure His creation eats. And when **the new day** begins to dawn, they go to their dens and nests and hidey **holes to sleep.** God gave them that instinct too.

Not many of us will encounter a lion in the wild. Bats **though, are a different story,** and they've frightened many a woman, man, **boy, and girl.** This evening, I hope you don't run into any unexpected **night creatures. But** I also hope you'll remember that God is providing for His **whole creation,** even through the night.

. . . .

Father, You make darkness and light; You made certain creatures for
day and some for night. Thank You for taking care of them all. Amen.

NIGHTTIME MEDITATIONS

I rise before the dawning of the morning, and cry for
help; I hope in Your word. My eyes are awake through the
night watches, that I may meditate on Your word.
PSALM 119:147–148 NKJV

Did this man ever sleep? As I read the Psalms, that's a question that arises. The psalmist repeatedly speaks of praising God day and night, of meditation at all hours, of worshipping at various times of day. How could a person be that engaged and energized?

There are a couple of possible explanations: one literal and one relational.

A literal interpretation would mean that the writer was basically awake and engaged all the time. This is highly unlikely, almost impossible physically and psychologically.

A relational interpretation means that the writer was in a state of passionate connection and communication with God, so much so that it *seemed* like a constant thing. He would talk to God during the day, offering praising while he went about his normal life. He could and would meditate in the evenings, and when he was awakened in the middle of the night, he would start talking to God again.

This is how the life of a true God-follower, a Christ-follower, should look. It is how your life can look, starting right now.

Lord God, I will talk to You at night and I will talk to You in the
morning. I am glad to be in relationship with You. Amen.

PROTECTED ALL THE TIME

The LORD is your keeper; the LORD is your shade at your right hand.
The sun shall not strike you by day, nor the moon by night.
PSALM 121:5–6 NKJV

Sunglasses and quilts. That's my twenty-first century analogy for this Bible passage.

Since my eyes are sensitive to the glare of the sun, I rely on sunglasses to protect them. At bedtime, I enjoy the warmth of a quilt—it protects against the cold.

In Psalm 121, an amazing passage of the Bible, we are promised that the Lord will be our protector. He will stand at our right hand, guarding us against both the blaze of the sun and the chill of the moon.

We need protection in our lives, both in the daytime and at night. The Lord promises to provide it—to an infinitely greater extent than sunglasses and quilts. He will protect our souls and preserve us for His glory.

Perhaps you're feeling alone tonight. Oh child, you are not! The Lord stands at your right side, and He is protecting you all the time.

. . . .

Lord, thank You for protecting me. I want You always by my side. Amen.

SURROUNDED

As the mountains surround Jerusalem, so the LORD
surrounds His people from this time forth and forever.
PSALM 125:2 NKJV

Pioneers in the American West were said to "circle the wagons" when threatened by enemies. From inside the circle, protected by the heavy wooden wagon bodies, the settlers would attempt to fight off attacks.

The 1953 John Wayne movie *Hondo* depicts this defensive maneuver but also the aggressive strategy of the Apache, who would "circle the circle"—riding their horses around the settlers' perimeter and cutting off any chance of escape.

I would imagine there's no worse feeling than knowing the enemy is on every side. But wouldn't it be nice to be surrounded by a superior force that's fighting for you? Or maybe I should say a superior force *who's* fighting for you.

Tonight, God says that *He* is surrounding you. He is in front of you and behind you, on either side of you, above you and beneath you. His presence and power are everywhere at once. And they are keeping you safe.

. . . .

God, I trust Your Word when it says that You
are surrounding me tonight. Amen.